How Much? How Fast?

Accumulated Change, Rates of Growth,
and the Fundamental Theorem of Calculus

Teacher's Guide

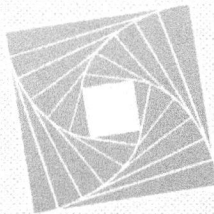

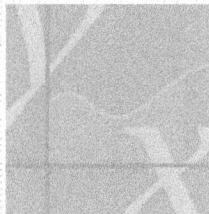

This material is based upon work supported by the National Science Foundation under award numbers ESI-9255262, ESI-0137805, and ESI-0627821. Any opinions, findings, and conclusions or recommendations expressed in this publication are those of the authors and do not necessarily reflect the views of the National Science Foundation.

Key Curriculum
1150 65th Street
Emeryville, California 94608
email: editorial@keypress.com
www.keycurriculum.com

First Edition Authors

Dan Fendel, Diane Resek, Lynne Alper, and Sherry Fraser

Contributors to the Second Edition

Sherry Fraser, Jean Klanica, Brian Lawler, Eric Robinson, Lew Romagnano, Rick Marks, Dan Brutlag, Alan Olds, Mike Bryant, Jeri P. Philbrick, Lori Green, Matt Bremer, Margaret DeArmond

Editor

Mali Apple

Editorial Assistant

Emily Reed

Professional Reviewer

Rick Marks, Sonoma State University

Math Checker

Carrie Gongaware

Production Editor

Andrew Jones

Production Director

Christine Osborne

Executive Editor

Josephine Noah

Mathematics Product Manager

Elizabeth DeCarli

Publisher

Steven Rasmussen

Contents

Blackline Masters

Calculator Guide and Calculator Notes

How Much? How Fast? Overview

Intent

This unit follows up on the previous development of the derivative of a function as a representation of instantaneous rate of change by looking at the issue of the *accumulation* of change. That is, if you have a graph or other means of describing the varying rate at which something is changing, how do you determine the *total change* over some interval? And what is the relationship between *how fast* a quantity is changing and *how much* it changes?

Mathematics

This unit focuses on key ideas and techniques from calculus and their applications in various settings. The main concepts and skills that students will encounter and practice during the unit are summarized below.

Accumulation
- Recognizing that the area under a rate curve represents an accumulation
- Estimating amount of total accumulation based on linear approximations of a situation
- Creating and analyzing graphs for accumulation as a function of time

Derivatives
- Reviewing the concept of a derivative as an instantaneous rate of change
- Estimating derivatives from graphs
- Developing formulas for derivatives of simple polynomial functions
- Developing formulas for derivatives of the sine and cosine functions
- Establishing principles for the derivative of a sum or constant multiple

The Fundamental Theorem of Calculus
- Seeing that an accumulation function is an antiderivative of the corresponding rate function
- Finding areas and volumes using antiderivatives

Trigonometry
- Defining radian measure
- Using radians in sine and cosine functions

Geometry
- Developing formulas for the volumes of pyramids and cones

IMP Year 4, *How Much? How Fast?* Unit, Teacher's Guide

© 2012 Interactive Mathematics Program

vi

Progression

The unit has two central problems. The first, *Building the Pyramid,* involves determining the volume of a pyramid and introduces the idea of approximation by easy-to-find pieces. The second, more complex problem, *Warming Up,* involves a solar energy collector. In the first phase of the problem, students do some trigonometric analysis to see how the energy is accumulating.

Ultimately, both problems are solved using a version of the fundamental theorem of calculus. The key idea, developed through a series of activities, is that the derivative of the function that describes *amount of accumulation* up to a particular time is simply the *rate of accumulation*. Put another way, the function describing the amount of accumulation (such as of volume or energy) is an *antiderivative* of the function describing the rate of accumulation.

As this principle is being developed, the concept of derivative is itself reviewed, and students extend their work from Year 3 to gain some facility finding derivatives of simple polynomial functions. They also extend their work in *The Diver Returns* with relationships among distance, speed, and acceleration.

Students then return to the pyramid problem, now through the more dynamic context of *Filling the Reservoir*, in which a pyramid-shaped reservoir is gradually being filled with water. They find a formula for the *rate* at which the reservoir is filled and apply the fundamental theorem of calculus to see that the total volume can be found using an antiderivative.

They then turn to the solar energy problem, first completing their analysis of the rate at which energy is accumulated. The formula for this rate involves the sine function, further extending ideas first developed in the Year 3 unit *High Dive* and in *The Diver Returns*. The balance of *How Much? How Fast?* is devoted to finding an antiderivative for this formula. This work includes introduction of radian measure for angles and finding the derivatives of the sine and cosine functions.

Adding Up the Parts: Using rate of growth and approximation to find total accumulation in several contexts; introducing the unit's POW

Rate and Accumulation: Reviewing and extending ideas about derivatives; finding formulas for derivatives of polynomials; establishing that the accumulation function is the antiderivative of the growth rate function

Pyramids and Energy: Solving the volume problem; introducing radian measure; developing a formula for the rate in the solar energy problem; finding derivatives and antiderivatives for sine and cosine; solving the solar energy problem

Pacing Guides

50-minute Pacing Guide (20 days)

Day	Activity	In-Class Time Estimate
1	Adding Up the Parts	0
	Building the Pyramid	50
	Homework: *How Far Did You Go?*	0
2	Discussion: *How Far Did You Go?*	10
	Another Trip	40
	Introduce: *POW 6: Advanced Pool Pockets*	0
	Homework: *How Fast? How Much?*	0
3	Discussion: *How Fast? How Much?*	15
	Leaky Faucet	30
	Reference: Units for Measuring Electricity	5
	Homework: *What's Watt?*	0
4	Discussion: *What's Watt?*	10
	Electrical Meter	40
	Homework: *Tilted Duct*	0
5	Discussion: *Tilted Duct*	10
	Warming Up	40
	Homework: *Total Heat*	0
6	Discussion: *Total Heat*	50
	Rate and Accumulation	0
	Homework: *How Fast Were You Going?*	0
7	Discussion: *How Fast Were You Going?*	15
	A Distance Graph	35
	Homework: *Let It Fall!*	0
8	Discussion: *Let It Fall!*	25
	Basic Derivatives	25
	Homework: *Summer Job*	0

9	Presentations and discussion: *POW 6: Advanced Pool Pockets*	15
	Basic Derivatives (continued)	15
	Discussion: *Summer Job*	20
	Homework: *Going Up?*	0
10	Discussion: *Going Up?*	10
	Down the Drain	40
	Homework: *Zero to Sixty*	0
11	Discussion: *Zero to Sixty*	20
	Polynomial Derivatives	30
	Homework: *Area and Distance*	0
12	Discussion: *Area and Distance*	10
	A Fundamental Relationship	40
	Homework: *The Leading Edge*	0
13	Discussion: *The Leading Edge*	10
	Pyramids and Energy	0
	Filling the Reservoir	40
	Homework: *A Pyramid of Bright Ideas*	0
14	Discussion: *A Pyramid of Bright Ideas*	10
	Trying a New Angle	40
	Homework: *Different Angles*	0
15	Discussion: *Different Angles*	15
	A Solar Formula	35
	Homework: *A Sine Derivative*	0
16	Discussion: *A Sine Derivative*	10
	A Derivative Proof	40
	Homework: *A Cosine Derivative*	0
17	Discussion: *A Cosine Derivative*	10
	The Inside Story	40
	Homework: *A Solar Summary*	0
18	Discussion: *A Solar Summary*	10

	"How Much? How Fast?" Portfolio	40
19	In-Class Assessment	40
	Homework: Take-Home Assessment (begin in class)	10
20	Exam Discussion	35
	Unit Reflection	15

IMP Year 4, *How Much? How Fast?* Unit, Teacher's Guide

x

© 2012 Interactive Mathematics Program

90-minute Pacing Guide (14 days)

Day	Activity	In-Class Time Estimate
1	Adding Up the Parts	0
	Building the Pyramid	45
	How Far Did You Go?	45
	Introduce: *POW 6: Advanced Pool Pockets*	0
	Homework: *Another Trip*	0
2	Discussion: *Another Trip*	10
	How Fast? How Much?	45
	Leaky Faucet	30
	Reference: Units for Measuring Electricity	5
	Homework: *What's Watt?*	0
3	Discussion: *What's Watt?*	10
	Electrical Meter	40
	Tilted Duct	40
	Homework: *Warming Up*	0
4	Discussion: *Warming Up*	15
	Total Heat	75
	Rate and Accumulation	0
	Homework: *How Fast Were You Going?*	0
5	Discussion: *How Fast Were You Going?*	20
	A Distance Graph	40
	Let It Fall!	30
	Homework: *POW 6: Advanced Pool Pockets*	0
6	Presentations and discussion: *POW 6: Advanced Pool Pockets*	20
	Let It Fall! (continued)	25
	Basic Derivatives	45
	Homework: *Summer Job*	0
7	Discussion: *Summer Job*	20

	Going Up?	40
	Down the Drain	30
	Homework: *Zero to Sixty*	0
8	*Down the Drain* (continued)	20
	Discussion: *Zero to Sixty*	20
	Polynomial Derivatives	40
	Homework: *Area and Distance* (begin in class)	10
9	Discussion: *Area and Distance*	10
	A Fundamental Relationship	45
	The Leading Edge	35
	Pyramids and Energy	0
	Homework: *Filling the Reservoir*	0
10	Discussion: *Filling the Reservoir*	15
	A Pyramid of Bright Ideas	35
	Trying a New Angle	40
	Homework: *Different Angles*	0
11	Discussion: *Different Angles*	15
	A Solar Formula	35
	A Sine Derivative	35
	Homework: *A Derivative Proof*	5
12	Discussion: *A Derivative Proof*	10
	A Cosine Derivative	35
	The Inside Story	45
	Homework: *A Solar Summary*	0
13	Discussion: *A Solar Summary*	10
	"How Much? How Fast?" Portfolio	40
	In-Class Assessment	40
	Homework: Take-Home Assessment	0
14	Exam Discussion	40
	Unit Reflection	15

IMP Year 4, *How Much? How Fast?* Unit, Teacher's Guide

© 2012 Interactive Mathematics Program

xii

Materials and Supplies

All IMP classrooms should have a set of standard supplies, described in the section "Materials and Supplies for the IMP Classroom" in A Guide to IMP. You'll also find a comprehensive list of materials needed for all Year 4 units in the section "Materials and Supplies for Year 4" in the Year 4 Teacher's Guide general resources.

Listed here are the supplies needed for this unit. Also available are general and activity-specific blackline masters, for transparencies or for student worksheets, in the "Blackline Masters" section in *How Much? How Fast?* Unit Resources.

How Much? How Fast? Materials

- Optional: Spreadsheet software
- Approximately 100 small cubical blocks for each group of students
- Grid poster paper

More About Supplies

Graph paper is a standard supply for IMP classrooms. Blackline masters of 1-Centimeter Graph Paper, 1/4-Inch Graph Paper, and 1-inch Graph Paper are provided, for you to make copies and transparencies.

IMP Year 4, *How Much? How Fast?* Unit, Teacher's Guide

xiii

© 2012 Interactive Mathematics Program

Assessing Progress

How Much? How Fast? concludes with two formal unit assessments. In addition, there are many opportunities for more informal, ongoing assessments throughout the unit. For more information about assessment and grading, including general information about the end-of-unit assessments and how to use them, consult *A Guide to IMP.*

End-of-Unit Assessments

This unit concludes with in-class and take-home assessments. The in-class assessment is intentionally short so that time pressures will not affect student performance. Students may use graphing calculators and their notes from previous work when they take the assessments. You can download unit assessments from the *How Much? How Fast?* Unit Resources.

Ongoing Assessment

One of the primary tasks of the classroom teacher is to assess student learning. Although the assigning of course grades may be part of this process, assessment more broadly includes the daily work of determining how well students understand key ideas and what level of achievement they have attained on key skills, in order to provide the best possible ongoing instructional program for them.

Students' written and oral work provides many opportunities for teachers to gather this information. We make some recommendations here of activities to monitor especially carefully that will give you insight into student progress.

- *Leaky Faucet*
- *A Distance Graph*
- *Zero to Sixty*
- *A Pyramid of Bright Ideas*
- *A Solar Summary*

Discussion of Unit Assessments

Have students volunteer to explain their work on each of the problems. Encourage questions and alternate explanations from other students.

In-Class Assessment

Have students share answers, emphasizing that they may have different explanations for Question 2.

IMP Year 4, *How Much? How Fast?* Unit, Teacher's Guide

xiv

© 2012 Interactive Mathematics Program

Take-Home Assessment

For Question 1a, students might note that the "average" value for the function is about 12, and the shaded area has a width of 3 units, so the area is around 36.

To get the area exactly, they will probably find an antiderivative for the function $y = x^3 - 2x^2 + 10$ and then substitute $x = 3$ into that antiderivative. If they use an antiderivative with a nonzero constant term, they would also substitute $x = 0$ and find the difference between the two results. (*Note:* The simplest antiderivative is $\dfrac{x^4}{4} - \dfrac{2x^3}{3} + 10x$, and substituting $t = 3$ gives an area of 32.25.)

For Question 2, if students use equal scales for the axes, they can estimate the slope from the graph, but they should also give an explanation. To explain their answer, they might compare the graph of $y = 3 \cos (2x)$ with the graph of $y = \cos x$.

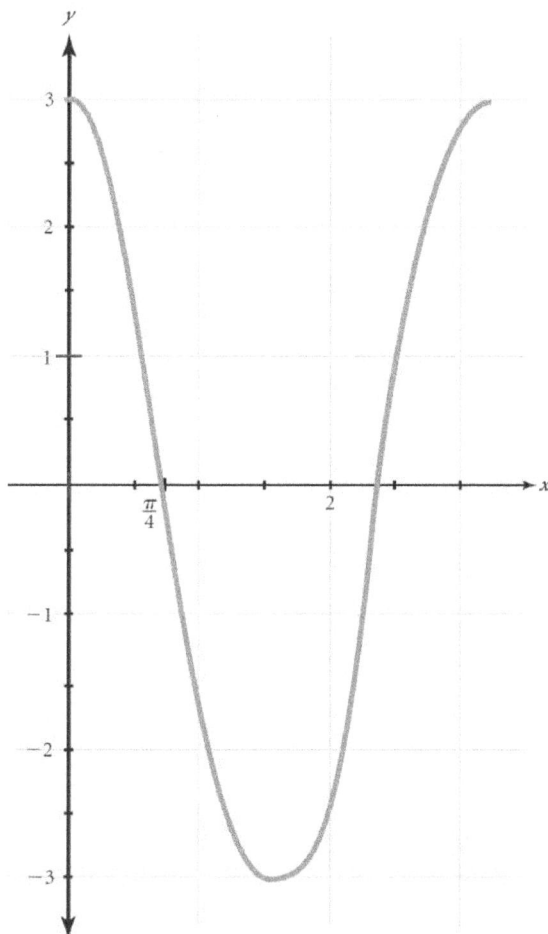

The graph of $y = 3 \cos (2x)$, shown here, can be obtained from the graph of $y = \cos x$ by "stretching" that graph vertically by a factor of 3 and "condensing" it horizontally by a factor of 2. In this comparison, the point $\left(\frac{\pi}{4}, 0\right)$ on the graph of $y = 3 \cos (2x)$ corresponds to the point $\left(\frac{\pi}{2}, 0\right)$ for the function $y = \cos x$.

Together, the stretching and shrinking factors mean that the graph of $y = 3 \cos (2x)$ is 6 times as steep at any given point as the other graph is at the corresponding point.

But for $y = \cos x$, the derivative is $y' = -\sin x$, so at $\left(\frac{\pi}{2}, 0\right)$, the derivative is -1. That means that for $y = 3 \cos (2x)$, the derivative at $\left(\frac{\pi}{4}, 0\right)$ is -6.

Supplemental Activities

The unit contains a variety of activities at the end of the student pages that you can use to supplement the regular unit material. These activities fall roughly into two categories.

- *Reinforcements* increase students' understanding and comfort with concepts, techniques, and methods that are discussed in class and are central to the unit.

- *Extensions* allow students to explore ideas beyond those presented in the unit, including generalizations and abstractions of ideas.

The supplemental activities are presented in the teacher's guide and the student book in the approximate sequence in which you might use them. Below are specific recommendations about how each activity might work within the unit. You may wish to use some of these activities, especially the later ones, after the unit is completed.

Derivative Power (extension) This activity extends students' study of derivatives, especially their work in *Basic Derivatives*.

Parabolic Area (reinforcement) In the discussion of *A Fundamental Relationship,* students saw the statement of the fundamental theorem of calculus, relating areas to antiderivatives. This activity follows up on that theorem with a specific example.

Ana on the Train (reinforcement) This activity blends an assortment of ideas from the unit—including accumulation, estimation, derivatives, and the fundamental theorem of calculus—into a single problem. You might assign this after students have reviewed their work so far in *A Pyramid of Bright Ideas*.

Widget Wisdom (extension) Following *The Inside Story*, students found an antiderivative for the solar energy rate function $P = 2400 \sin\left(\frac{\pi}{12}t\right)$, which involved adjusting for the "inside coefficient" $\frac{\pi}{12}$ and the "outside coefficient" 2400. In this activity, students examine the issue of such coefficients through a productivity function, $w = f(t)$. They look at two related productivity functions, which might be expressed as $y_1 = 2f(t)$ and $y_2 = f(3t)$, and examine how they compare with the original function in terms of graphs and derivatives.

Adding Up the Parts

Intent

These activities introduce the concept of accumulation graphs and their relationship to rate graphs.

Mathematics

In these activities, students examine the relationships between **rate graphs** and **accumulation graphs.** They see that the area under a speed curve represents distance traveled and that, in general, the area under a rate curve represents an accumulation. They also observe that the slope of an accumulation graph corresponds to the rate of accumulation.

Progression

Building the Pyramid introduces the first of two central problems for this unit: finding the volume of a pyramid. After students estimate the solution to this problem, the activities leave the pyramid for a while to develop some of the principles they will need to find an exact answer.

How Far Did You Go? reminds students that the area under a speed curve represents distance traveled, and *Another Trip* adds the complication of estimating the area under a speed curve when there is nonlinear acceleration. This situation is developed further in *How Fast? How Much?*, where students construct an accumulation graph.

Students see rate and accumulation graphs in another context in *Leaky Faucet*, as they begin to look more closely at the relationships between these two types of graphs. A sequence of activities then leads to introduction of the second central problem for the unit, in *Warming Up. Units for Measuring Electricity* introduces watts and watt-hours, which will be used in *What's Watt?* in preparation for *Warming Up.* This problem, continued in *Total Heat*, involves the accumulation of energy by a solar-collection panel and provides, in a very different context, another look at the relationships between rate and accumulation graphs.

Building the Pyramid
How Far Did You Go?
Another Trip
POW 6: Advanced Pool Pockets
How Fast? How Much?
Leaky Faucet
What's Watt?
Electrical Meter

Tilted Duct
Warming Up
Total Heat

Building the Pyramid

Intent

This activity introduces the first of the two central unit problems.

Mathematics

In this activity, students estimate the volume of a pyramid using intuitive methods. (The unit does not assume that students know a formula for the volume.) They will return to the problem near the end of the unit with new tools for getting an exact volume and a general formula.

Progression

Students estimate the volume of a given pyramid by using cubes to model several pyramids and then extending the patterns they observe in their data. The subsequent discussion examines the variety of approaches students used and focuses on ways their estimates could be improved. The class saves the estimates for comparison later in the unit.

Approximate Time

45 to 50 minutes

Classroom Organization

Small groups, followed by whole-class discussion

Materials

Approximately 100 small cubical blocks for each group of students
Optional: Spreadsheet software

Doing the Activity

If some students know the formula for the volume of a pyramid, have them do this activity without using it (although they might use it to check their answers). You might mention that the class will develop the formula and learn an explanation for why it works by the end of the unit.

After students have read the activity, ask, What makes it difficult to model a true pyramid with cubes? Finding the volume of a true pyramid is tricky because a true pyramid has sloping sides. Students are to approximate the sloping slides using cubes.

Provide sets of cubes, and suggest that groups build some approximations for simpler cases, such as a pyramid that is 6 cubes high with a 6-by-6 base.

Once students have figured out that a sum of squares is mathematically appropriate, they could easily construct spreadsheet tables like the one below to show the relevant quantities, compare the results to their hand-generated data, and extend them to approximate the solution.

Height	Volume of new layer	Total volume
1	1	1
2	4	5
3	9	14
4	16	30
5	25	55
6	36	91
...	...	...

If spreadsheet software is not available, students could generate similar tables (though with more effort) using lists or matrices on their calculators and summation functions. Or they could write a simple calculator program to find the total volume, though in this case they could not directly observe the growth patterns. The most basic approach is to calculate the sum $100^2 + 99^2 + 98^2 + \ldots + 2^2 + 1^2$ step by step.

Discussing and Debriefing the Activity

Students have some choices to make in developing an approximation, and it's useful to elicit several ideas. How did your group model the 100-foot-high pyramid? One natural option, used here for discussion purposes, is to make a first layer that is 100 by 100, then place a 99-by-99 layer on top of it, and so on, for 100 layers, with the top layer made up of a single block. This gives a volume of $100^2 + 99^2 + 98^2 + \ldots + 2^2 + 1^2$. (*Note:* A common error is to make the second layer 98 by 98, one layer "in" from the edge. Continuing like this will give a pyramid that is only 50 units high.)

If some students have made their approximation using $100^2 + 99^2 + 98^2 + \ldots + 2^2 + 1^2$, you might ask, How does your approximation compare with the volume of the actual pyramid? They should see that it is larger, but assure them that it is a good estimate.

Some students might instead use an "empty" top row and a 99-by-99 bottom row to get $99^2 + 98^2 + \ldots + 1^2 + 0^2$. If so, ask, **How does this approximation compare with the exact value? How might we use the two estimates together to get an even better approximation?** Students will probably recognize that the average of the underestimate and the overestimate will be better than either by itself. (For your information, the sum $100^2 + 99^2 + 98^2 + \ldots + 2^2 + 1^2$ is 338,350. The volume of the actual pyramid is $\frac{1,000,000}{3} = 333,333.33$, so the approximation is off by less than 2%. Averaging the "too large" and the "too small" estimates gives 333,350, which is off by less than a hundredth of a percent.)

You might also ask, **How else could we get a better approximation? Could we modify our model in a way that would provide a better approximation of a true pyramid?** One approach is to use smaller cubes, such as cubes 0.5 foot on each side. If students try this, be alert for the mistake of still using only 100 layers of cubes. Experimenting with different cube sizes is greatly simplified by using a spreadsheet to do the calculations.

Save the approximations found today for comparison with the exact value, to be found using calculus later in the unit (see *Filling the Reservoir*).

Key Questions

What makes it difficult to model a true pyramid with cubes?
How did your group model the 100-foot-high pyramid?
How does your approximation compare with the volume of the actual pyramid?
How could we combine more than one model to obtain a better approximation for the pyramid's volume?
How else could we get a better approximation? Could we modify our model in a way that would provide a better approximation of a true pyramid?

How Far Did You Go?

Intent

Students use a graph of a car's speed versus time to find distance traveled.

Mathematics

This activity is similar to *Building the Pyramid,* as it involves getting a total by adding up parts of the total and students might use estimation. As students work, they recall that the area under a speed curve represents the distance traveled. They also review the principle that for a period of constant acceleration, the average speed is the average of the initial and final speeds.

Progression

Students determine how far a car traveled given a graph of a car's speed over time. The subsequent discussion reviews that for constant speeds, distance traveled is equal to rate times time. It also reviews the method of using the area under the speed graph to find the distance traveled.

During the discussion of *Total Heat*, students will make another graph from this information, showing the distance traveled as a function of time. For now, they have been asked only for the total distance. Save the results from this activity for use in constructing that later graph (see the section "Accumulation Graphs").

Approximate Time

25 to 35 minutes for activity (at home or in class)
10 minutes for discussion

Classroom Organization

Individuals, followed by whole-class discussion

Doing the Activity

You might remind students that they did a very similar activity (*Distance with Changing Speed*) in the unit *The Diver Returns*.

If students ask about the near-vertical segments in the graph, explain that they indicate that the car needs some time to speed up and slow down, but that students can treat them as if they were purely vertical, that is, as if the car started up at full speed or came to sudden stops.

Discussing and Debriefing the Activity

Begin the discussion by having several students explain how they computed the total distance traveled. **How is distance calculated from speed and time? What does that calculation represent in terms of the geometry of the speed graph?**

Be sure students understand that for time intervals of constant speed, the distance traveled is the product of the speed and the length of the time interval. Use this idea to establish the principle that, at least for the sections with constant speed, the distance over the time interval is numerically equal to the area under the graph for that section. These areas are rectangles in which the horizontal dimension is the length of time interval and the vertical dimension is the speed.

Ask, **Does this area principle apply for time intervals with nonconstant speed?** Help students to see that these intervals can be broken up into very short time periods. These short time periods are like intervals with constant speed, so the area principle still applies.

As students use the area principle, ask about the units involved in each dimension. For instance, if they use the grid, each box is "0.5 hour wide" and "5 miles per hour" high, giving an area of 2.5 miles.

Note that "area" in this discussion actually represents length, because it gives the distance the car has traveled. You might ask the class, **Why is one-dimensional distance (length) represented by two-dimensional area?**

With this area principle established, there are several ways to find the total distance, including these:

- Counting boxes (using the grid to estimate the area)
- Finding each portion of the total area as a trapezoid (which is equivalent to treating each time segment as if it has a constant speed that is the average of the speeds at each end of the time segment)
- Estimating for each segment (essentially, using short intervals and treating each time segment as if it involves a constant speed)

Students should get a total of approximately 125 miles for the distance traveled.

Key Questions

How is distance calculated from speed and time? What does that calculation represent in terms of the geometry of the speed graph? Does the area principle apply for time intervals with nonconstant speed? Why is one-dimensional distance (length) represented by two-dimensional area?

Another Trip

Intent

Students use a graph of speed with nonlinear acceleration to estimate distance traveled.

Mathematics

Although the question in this activity is essentially the same as in *How Far Did You Go?*, nonlinear acceleration makes the task much more difficult. The key is realizing that the area under the speed curve still represents the distance traveled, but now students must estimate that area.

Progression

Given a graph of a curve representing a car's changing speed over an interval of time, students find the distance traveled by estimating the area under the curve.

Approximate Time

30 minutes for activity (at home or in class)
10 minutes for discussion

Classroom Organization

Individuals or small groups, followed by whole-class discussion

Doing the Activity

If students explore the activity in groups, you might suggest that different group members work on different time periods and pool their results.

Discussing and Debriefing the Activity

As students present their analyses, emphasize that even though this graph has no time periods with constant speed, the area under the curve still represents the total distance traveled.

After discussing the solutions, ask, How could you get a more accurate estimate? Students are likely to see that subdividing the time intervals into smaller segments might help. They might also see an analogy with the idea of using smaller blocks to estimate the volume of the pyramid in *Building the Pyramid*.

You might ask for a "15-second way" to estimate the distance. **How could you get a quick estimate of the total distance?** The intent is to have students estimate, roughly, what horizontal line would give the same area as there is under the curve. Students should see that a line at about 54 miles per hour might work, so that the overall distance for the 2-hour trip is about 108 miles.

Key Questions

How could you get a more accurate estimate?
How could you get a quick estimate of the total distance?

POW 6: Advanced Pool Pockets

Intent

Students work from specific cases toward increasing levels of generalization and then justify their results.

Mathematics

A basic solution to this problem uses the greatest common factor, while a more advanced analysis involves the least common multiple and the definitions of rational and irrational numbers.

Progression

Give students about a week to work on this POW. Presentations will follow.

Approximate Time

3 to 4 hours for activity (at home)
15 to 20 minutes for presentations and discussion

Classroom Organization

Individuals, followed by whole-class presentations and discussion

Doing the Activity

On the day before the POW is due, select three students to make presentations on the following day.

Discussing and Debriefing the Activity

You might encourage presenters to discuss particular cases first and then show how they lead to more general solutions. Sequences or tables of numbers show some patterns quickly for whole numbers. Students may have generated specific formulas for the number of bounces in the cases where the length and width are relatively prime, where one is a multiple of the other, and where both share a factor greater than 1 but less than the smaller dimension. If no one demonstrates a single formula encompassing all three cases, you might ask students to consider whether one is possible. Similar analysis leads to some general conclusions about which pocket the ball finally reaches.

Non-whole-number Dimensions

The activity does not specify that the dimensions be whole numbers. If one or both dimensions are rational numbers but not integers, an additional step can reduce the situation to a whole-number case.

If no one mentions it, ask, **What would happen if one of the dimensions were an irrational number?** The ensuing discussion and surprising conclusion should reinforce the definition of an *irrational number* as a number that can never be represented as the ratio of two integers.

How Fast? How Much?

Intent

Students explore rate relationships and are introduced to the connection between rate graphs and accumulation graphs.

Mathematics

Students generalize the relationship

$$\text{Amount} = \text{Rate} \times \text{Time}$$

to a variety of contexts, including those in which the "per unit" variable is not time. The rates are always determined as constants. The last question connects the relations to their graphs. This activity and the follow-up activity help students see that this sort of relation can be viewed in two different but complementary ways, as a **rate graph** or as an **accumulation graph.**

Progression

In several rate problems involving constant rates, students specify the rate, the variables, and their units; write an equation; and use the equation to solve the problem. They then make up similar problems of their own, describe the general form that all the problems share, and graph two of the equations. The subsequent discussion includes construction of additional graphs for several problems in which the rate is on the vertical axis. The area under the graph is identified as the accumulated amount.

Approximate Time

30 minutes for activity (at home or in class)
15 minutes for discussion

Classroom Organization

Individuals, then small groups, followed by whole-class discussion

Doing the Activity

You might point out that the equations could be set up in more than one way (proportions would be a reasonable form, for instance), but that the instructions request that one variable be written as a function of another.

If students say these are simple problems suitable for Year 1, assure them the discussion will touch on some new ideas.

Discussing and Debriefing the Activity

Have students share the problems they made up for Question 2 in their groups. Use this to lead into a discussion of rate. Emphasize the units associated with each rate, and make the general notion more explicit: What are the units of the constant rate? What are the units of the variables? What is a rate? Be sure students recognize that although many rates are with respect to time, many are not.

Choose three or four problems and ask as many students to put their equations and graphs on the board, leaving a little room next to each. Then have volunteers refer to these examples to explain their answers to Questions 3 and 4. If some of their equations are in the form of proportions, ask, How could you convert this proportion into a functional form involving a rate?

It may happen that students translate a single problem into two different rate equations. For instance, Question 1g could result in $A = 450G$ (where the rate is 450 square feet per gallon) or $G = \frac{1}{450}A$ (where the rate is $\frac{1}{450}$ gallon per square foot). Both forms are meaningful and useful, and both belong to the class of functions under consideration.

Now assign students the task of making a second graph for each of the problems on the board. These graphs should again have the independent variable on the horizontal axis, but the *rate* on the vertical axis. Insist that students label quantities clearly, including units. When ready, have a few students put the rate graphs on the board next to their corresponding initial graphs.

These **rate graphs** should all show constant functions.

This next question targets the key idea in this activity: How could you use these rate graphs to solve the problems directly? For a given value of the independent variable, the corresponding rectangular area under the graph represents the accumulated amount of the dependent quantity. Encourage students to articulate why this makes sense in terms of the quantities involved. Bring out also the "multiplication and cancellation" of units; this process of *unit analysis* is very useful in scientific calculations. Note how these relationships generalize to *all* problems involving constant rates, regardless of the specific units.

Some students may begin to connect, or wonder about, the relationship between these two ways of solving the same problems. This could serve as a natural lead-in to the next activity, which explores this relationship in some detail.

Key Questions

What are the units of the constant rate? What are the units of the variables? What is a rate?
How could you use these rate graphs to solve the problems directly?

Leaky Faucet

Intent

Students construct a rate graph and an accumulation graph for the same situation and then explore the relationships between the two graphs.

Mathematics

This activity helps students begin to recognize some of the connections that will enable them to understand the **fundamental theorem of calculus.** The activity requires them to articulate the fact that the slope of an accumulation graph at any point in time is equal to the value of the rate at the same point in time on the related rate graph. They also verbalize the relationship between the area under a rate graph up to a point in time and the corresponding value for the same point in time on an accumulation graph.

Progression

Students construct rate and accumulation graphs for a situation involving constant rates that are different over each of several time intervals. They then describe how the graphs are related, in terms of both the rate and the accumulation. The subsequent discussion focuses on these relationships, which relate to the essence of the fundamental theorem of calculus, the big mathematical idea in this unit.

Approximate Time

30 minutes

Classroom Organization

Individuals, followed by whole-class discussion

Doing the Activity

After their recent work, students should have no trouble completing the graphs on their own, though they may struggle with articulating the relationships.

Discussing and Debriefing the Activity

Students will see that the graph for Question 1 consists of three horizontal line segments and the graph for Question 2 consists of three nonhorizontal line segments. They should be able to explain why one graph is essentially flat while the other is always rising.

IMP Year 4, *How Much? How Fast?* Unit, Teacher's Guide

© 2012 Interactive Mathematics Program

15

If necessary for Question 3, ask, **How is the rate of the drip represented on the graph for Question 1? How is it represented on the graph for Question 2?** The key idea here is that the slope of each line segment from the second graph is the value of the first graph (which is the rate) for that time period. For instance, in the second graph, the segment representing the first 40 minutes should have a slope of 10, which is the height of the corresponding horizontal segment of the graph in Question 1. This value, 10, is the rate (in milliliters per minute) at which the water is dripping during that time period.

Students' previous work should enable them to answer Question 4, calculating the area under the first graph (the rate) up to a given time and seeing that it matches the corresponding value on the second graph (the accumulation). If necessary, ask, **How is the amount of water in the bucket represented on the graph for Question 1? How is it represented on the graph for Question 2?** Then ask students to calculate the accumulation at a few specific times and then to generalize the relationship.

Key Questions

How is the rate of the drip represented on the graph for Question 1? How is it represented on the graph for Question 2?
How is the amount of water in the bucket represented on the graph for Question 1? How is it represented on the graph for Question 2?

Units for Measuring Electricity

Intent

Students are introduced to the measurement units that will be used in *What's Watt?*

Mathematics

This reference page introduces two units used to measure electricity: watts and watt-hours.

Progression

The reference page summarizes information that will be applied in *What's Watt?* in preparation for *Warming Up.*

Approximate Time

5 minutes

Classroom Organization

Whole-class discussion

Doing the Activity

The reference page explains the units used to measure electricity, which can be confusing. You may wish to answer any questions about them before students begin the activity *What's Watt?*

IMP Year 4, *How Much? How Fast?* Unit, Teacher's Guide

© 2012 Interactive Mathematics Program

17

What's Watt?

Intent

Students get familiar with the measurement units that will be used in *Warming Up.*

Mathematics

This activity makes use of two units used to measure electricity: watts and watt-hours.

Progression

Students make a graph showing the rate at which energy is being consumed in a household in which lamps of various wattages are turned on and off throughout the day. They then find the total amount of energy used by the lamps in one day.

Approximate Time

30 minutes for activity (at home or in class)
10 minutes for discussion

Classroom Organization

Individuals, followed by whole-class discussion

Doing the Activity

Students may want to refer to the reference page **Units for Measuring Electricity** as they work on this activity.

Discussing and Debriefing the Activity

Before discussing the questions, you may want to review the key idea that watts measure the *rate* of electricity usage. This is confusing, because most units measuring rates appear in "something per something" form. In this field, that form is joules per second, but the more common name for this unit is *watts*. So the graph that students constructed for Question 1 is really a rate graph.

For Question 1, the key is to keep track of which lamps are on at which times. Here is a summary by time:
- Midnight–7 a.m.: one 60-watt lamp (total: 60 watts)
- 7 a.m.–9 a.m.: one 60-watt lamp plus three 100-watt lamps (total: 360 watts)

- 9 a.m.–3 p.m.: one 60-watt lamp, three 100-watt lamps, and five 150-watt lamps (total: 1110 watts)
- 3 p.m.–6 p.m.: one 60-watt lamp and five 150-watt lamps (total: 810 watts)
- 6 p.m.–8 p.m.: one 60-watt lamp (total: 60 watts)
- 8 p.m.–10 p.m.: one 60-watt lamp and two 200-watt lamps (total: 460 watts)
- 10 p.m.–midnight: one 60-watt lamp (total: 60 watts)

Thus, the rate graph looks like this:

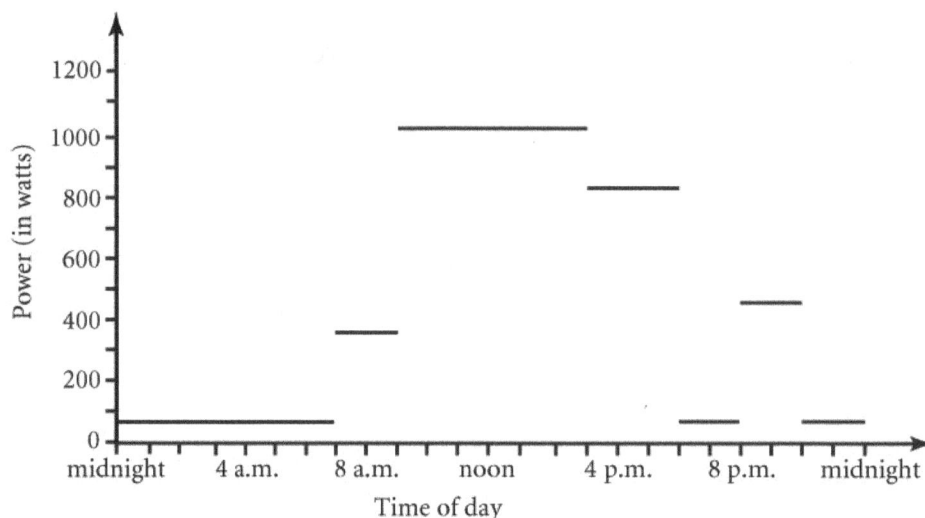

You might mention the term *step function* to describe a graph that consists of a series of horizontal line segments. Note that this particular graph is not really a function, since at several times (such as 7 a.m.) it shows two different power levels. This situation cannot arise physically; the change in power is nearly instantaneous but not quite. Mathematical models typically account for this by graphing open circles at one of the two conflicting endpoints, though this refinement of the graph is not necessary for the current purposes.

For Question 2, here are two approaches:

- Multiply the length of each time period by the power for that time period:

  $60 \cdot 7 + 360 \cdot 2 + 1110 \cdot 6 + 810 \cdot 3 + 60 \cdot 2 + 460 \cdot 2 + 60 \cdot 2$

  This gives a total of 11,390 watt-hours, or 11.39 kilowatt-hours.
  If students do this calculation without reference to the graph, ask, How could you use the graph to find the total energy usage? This reminds them that they are working with a rate graph and reinforces the area approach to calculating amount, or accumulation.
- Treat each bulb separately. The 60-watt bulb burns for 24 hours, the three 100-watt bulbs each burn for 8 hours, and so on. The total could then be computed by this expression:

  $60 \cdot 24 + 3 \cdot 100 \cdot 8 + 5 \cdot 150 \cdot 9 + 2 \cdot 200 \cdot 2$

As a follow-up, you might ask, **What wattage would be needed for a single bulb burning all day (and night) to use the same total amount of electricity?** The simplest approach is to divide the total energy consumption by 24. Another is to look for a horizontal line on the graph that seems about average. Students should see that the area under this "average consumption" line equals the area under the step function from Question 1. You might point out that the energy-consumption graph never actually takes on this average value.

Key Questions

How could you use the graph to find the total energy usage?
What wattage would be needed for a single bulb burning all day (and night) to use the same total amount of electricity?

Electrical Meter

Intent

Students create another accumulation graph and again examine the relationships between the rate and accumulation graphs.

Mathematics

Students use the information from *What's Watt?* to create an accumulation graph. This activity gives them a second example, in addition to *Leaky Faucet*, of describing the accumulation process as a function of time. They then consider how rate is represented in the rate graph and in the accumulation graph.

Progression

Students construct an accumulation graph of the data in *What's Watt?* The subsequent discussion brings out the connection between rates in the original graph and slopes in the accumulation graph.

Approximate Time

40 minutes

Classroom Organization

Small groups or individuals, followed by whole-class discussion

Doing the Activity

Be sure students recognize that they need to use a different vertical scale from the graph they drew for *What's Watt?* Even if students are working in groups, they should all make their own graphs.

Discussing and Debriefing the Activity

The accumulation graph will look something like this:

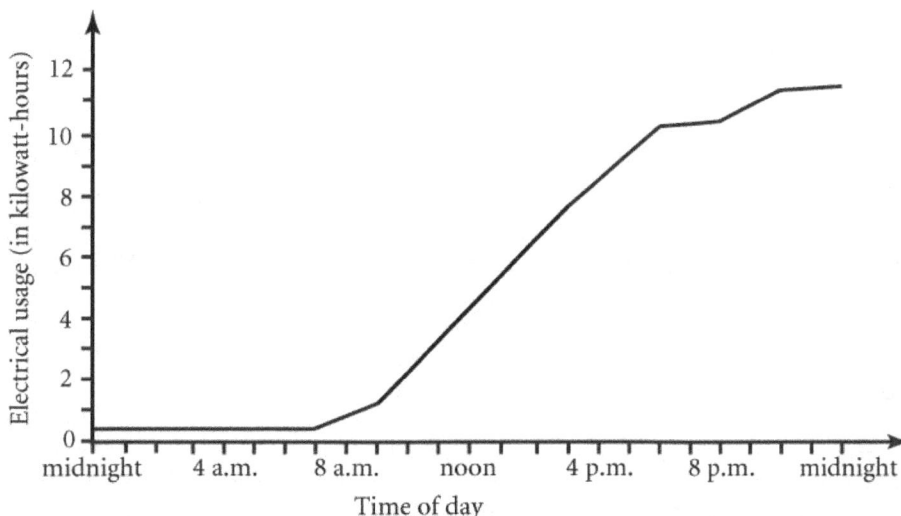

After the graph has been presented and explained, ask, **How is this new graph related to the graph from *What's Watt?*** Several observations should come from this discussion. Students might first notice that their new graph has a final value (11.39 kilowatt-hours) that is equal to the total amount of electricity used, as found in *What's Watt?*

To bring out the second point, ask, **Why are all the parts of this graph straight line segments?** Students should recognize that this is because the original graph is made up of horizontal segments. That is, for each of several time intervals, the electricity-use *rate* is constant. Therefore, when the *accumulated amount* of electricity consumed is considered as a function of time during any of those time intervals, that function is *increasing* at a constant rate and therefore forms a linear graph.

Third, ask, **What determines how fast this graph rises?** Students should see that the slope of each segment of the new graph is equal to the height of the original graph during the given time period. This observation will help lay the groundwork for the eventual recognition that the derivative of an accumulation graph is the rate graph from which it was formed.

Key Questions

How is this new graph related to the graph from *What's Watt?*
Why are all the parts of this graph straight line segments?
What determines how fast this graph rises?

Tilted Duct

Intent

Students examine a situation that will prepare them to address the second central unit problem.

Mathematics

Warming Up features a solar panel collecting energy from the sun. As the sun moves across the sky, the rate of energy collection varies as a sine function. Many people find it difficult to understand the optics of the situation. In particular, they have trouble envisioning the sun's rays as parallel and how this affects the intensity when those rays meet the absorbing surface at an angle.

In *Tilted Duct,* students examine a similar but simpler situation that leads to a cosine function. After solving this easier problem, they should be more able to make sense of the solar situation.

Progression

Students use trigonometry to analyze rainfall collection in preparation for understanding solar energy collection in the next activity.

Approximate Time

30 minutes for activity (at home or in class)
10 minutes for discussion

Classroom Organization

Individuals, followed by whole-class discussion

Doing the Activity

This activity requires no introduction.

Discussing and Debriefing the Activity

A key feature of this problem is that, with no wind, rain falls vertically. Carefully drawn diagrams will reveal that the cosine of the angle of tilt is a multiplier that gradually reduces the amount of rain entering the tilted duct and that this reduction intensifies as the angle increases.

After students share solutions to this problem, you may want to just move on to the next activity and let students figure out later how the rain-collector ideas might be useful in analyzing the solar-collector problem.

Warming Up

Intent

This activity introduces the second central unit problem.

Mathematics

Students analyze a situation in which a solar-collection panel absorbs energy over the course of a day to understand the rate at which energy is absorbed. In *Total Heat,* they will use that analysis to get data about the energy accumulated as a function of time. In the subsequent discussion, they will graph those data.

Progression

Students draw a graph showing the rate at which the solar panel absorbs energy, given that the rate of energy accumulation varies with the angle of incidence. Students save their results, as well as make posters of their graphs, for reference in *Total Heat* and later in the unit.

In *A Solar Formula,* students will develop an equation for the graph for the period from 6 a.m. to 6 p.m. as a function of time. If they seem interested, you might have them do that now, but in the later activity, they will work with radian measure for angles, so they would have to adjust any work they do now.

Approximate Time

30 minutes for activity (at home or in class)
10 to 20 minutes for discussion and making posters

Classroom Organization

Small groups or individuals, followed by whole-class discussion

Materials

Grid poster paper

Doing the Activity

As with *Building the Pyramid,* students start with an estimate and then return later in the unit (in several activities, beginning with *A Pyramid of Bright Ideas*) to get a more precise answer. As you introduce the activity, you may want to mention that long-term plan and explain that students will be making posters in the next two activities for later reference.

Students may be able to use their experience in *Tilted Duct* to figure out the role of the angle in changing the intensity (and thus the energy) of light striking the panel. If not, you may need to provide considerable guidance. The discussion notes give details about a possible analysis.

After students figure out the graph, have them each save the result for use in *Total Heat* as well as later in the unit. Then have them work in their groups to make a poster of the graph. These posters, together with those made for *Total Heat*, will serve as referents for the more analytical work on this problem, beginning in *A Pyramid of Bright Ideas*.

Discussing and Debriefing the Activity

One way to do the basic analysis is with a diagram like this one, shown for 10 a.m., when the angle of the sun is 60°.

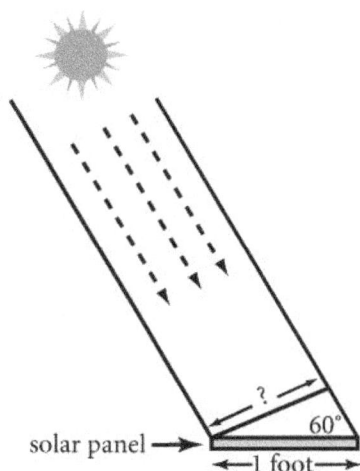

As the sun's rays (the arrows) go toward the 1-foot-square solar panel, the width of the band of rays that hits the panel is less than 1 foot wide. The actual width is labeled "?" in the diagram.

Basic trigonometry shows that this width (in feet) is sin 60°. Therefore, the intensity of the sun's rays at 10 a.m. must be multiplied by sin 60°, or about .866.

Another approach to the analysis is with a vector decomposition of the sun's rays, using ideas developed in *The Diver Returns*. That is, one can think of the sun's rays as having vertical and horizontal components. Only the vertical component affects the solar panel (since the horizontal component is parallel to the panel's surface), and that component can be found by multiplying the full amount by sin 60°.

In general, the amount of power (in watts) per square foot of panel is 80 sin θ, where θ is the angle at which the sun's rays hit the panel. In the diagram, this angle is 60°. Because there are 30 square feet of panels, the rate at which energy is being absorbed for the entire system, as a function of θ, is given by the equation $P = 2400 \sin \theta$.

From midnight until 6 a.m. the sun has not appeared, so the graph is horizontal, at $y = 0$. During this time period, the angle θ has no meaning. The angle then goes from 0° at 6 a.m. up to a maximum of 90° at noon, and then back to 0° (or continuing up to 180°) at 6 p.m. Over this interval, the graph forms the "upper hump" of a sine curve. From 6 p.m. until midnight, the graph is horizontal again, at $y = 0$.

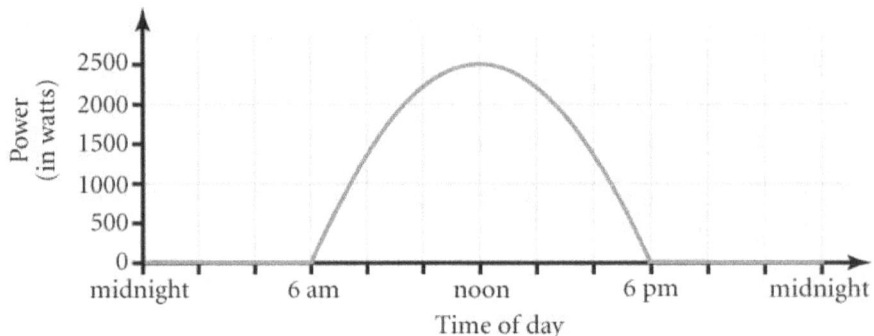

You may want to remind students that they will need their results from this activity for *Total Heat*.

Total Heat

Intent

Students use estimates of the area beneath the curve in a rate graph to construct an accumulation graph.

Mathematics

This activity leads into a summary of the concept of an **accumulation graph.**

Progression

Students use the graph from *Warming Up* to estimate the total energy absorbed by the solar collector during each of several time periods, the total energy accumulated throughout the day to the end of each time period, and the total energy collected during the day. In the subsequent discussion, they make accumulation graphs from their results, and groups then make posters of the graphs. The class discusses the idea of an accumulation graph, paying special attention to what is "accumulating" in each of several earlier problems. Students then make an accumulation graph for the situation from *How Far Did You Go?*

Approximate Time

30 minutes for activity (at home or in class)
45 to 50 minutes for discussion and making posters

Classroom Organization

Individuals, followed by whole-class discussion and small groups

Materials

Grid poster paper

Doing the Activity

You may want to remind students that they will need their results from *Warming Up* for this activity.

Discussing and Debriefing the Activity

Students' work in *Electrical Meter* should direct them toward the idea that the area beneath the curve represents the total energy accumulated. As they did for similar activities (*How Far Did You Go?* and *Another Trip*), they are likely to use various methods to estimate this area.

In the graph below and in the discussion notes for *Warming Up*, each box has a width of 2 hours and a height of 1000 watts and thus represents 2 kilowatt-hours. Consequently, the area under the graph from 6 a.m. to 8 a.m. (for instance) is about 0.6 box, and therefore represents about 1.2 kilowatt-hours.

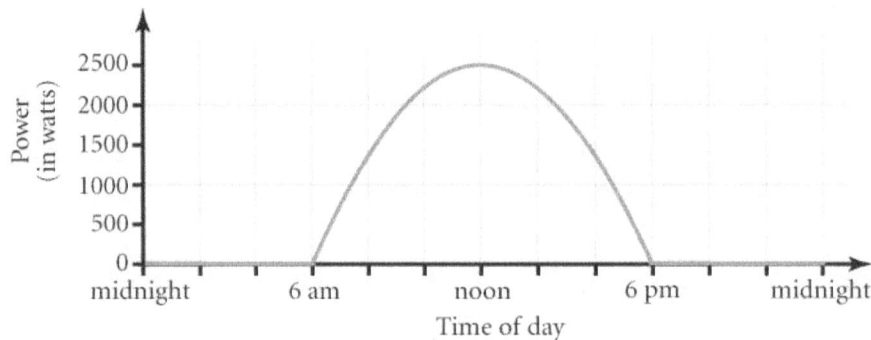

Some students might use the graph's symmetry to ease the work, recognizing that the energy accumulation for the periods from noon to 6 p.m. equal those of similar periods from 6 a.m. to noon.

Continuing this way might give these estimates:

Time interval	Energy (in kilowatt-hours) absorbed during the interval	Total energy (in kilowatt-hours) absorbed from midnight to the end of the interval
Midnight to 6 a.m.	0	0
6 a.m. to 8 a.m.	1.2	1.2
8 a.m. to 10 a.m.	3.4	4.6
10 a.m. to noon	4.6	9.2
Noon to 2 p.m.	4.6	13.8
2 p.m. to 4 p.m.	3.4	17.2
4 p.m. to 6 p.m.	1.2	18.4
6 p.m. to midnight	0	18.4

The resulting total energy accumulation is 18.4 kilowatt-hours. You might ask students to compare this total with using 1200 watts (half the maximum) as the average rate for the 12-hour period, perhaps even suggesting that maybe the total should actually be 14.4 kilowatt-hours (12 hours times 1.2 kilowatts). This might get them to articulate that using the "middle value" as the average is only legitimate if the quantity in question is changing at a constant rate.

Have students plot the values from the final column of their table as a function of time. The result should look something like this:

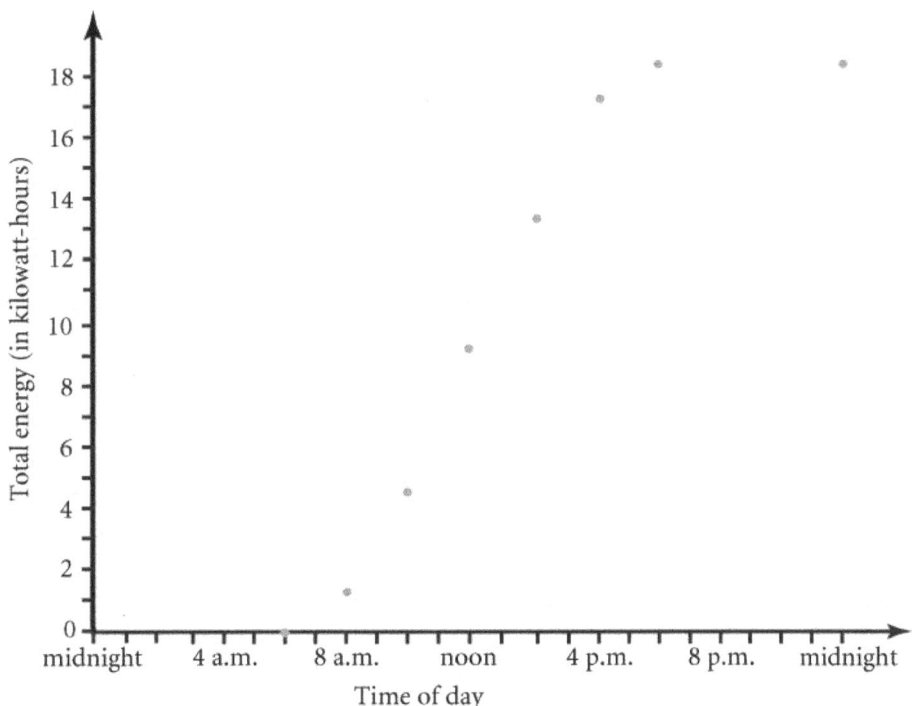

You might then ask, **Does this graph look like anything you know?** Focus students' attention on the portion between 6 a.m. and 6 p.m. If they don't recognize this as similar to a sine graph, that's fine for now.

After students have completed their graphs, again have groups make posters for later reference. Tell students to save their results from this activity. They will review their current findings in *A Pyramid of Bright Ideas*, when they return to the solar panel problem, and in subsequent activities.

Watts as a Unit of Power

Students may continue to be confused about watts as a unit of power, as rates are usually expressed as a ratio of one variable quantity to a second variable quantity (often time). *How Fast? How Much?* reinforced the concept of multiplying the rate by this second quantity to find the accumulation, or the area under the rate graph. Watts combine the ratio into a single value, so they do not appear to measure a rate.

If this still seems to stump students, you might construct another version of the power graph from *Warming Up* using joules/hour as the unit of power. (A watt is defined to be 1 joule per second, so 1 watt = 3600 J/hr). The amplitude then becomes 8,640,000 J/hr, and it makes sense to multiply these units by hours to calculate accumulated energy. To reverse the conversion, note that 3600 joules = 1 watt-hour.

Later in the unit, students will see that the area under a graph can be found using the antiderivative of the function defining the graph. Using this approach, they will get an exact value for the total energy absorbed for the day.

Accumulation Graphs

This is a good time to synthesize students' work in the past several activities. You could begin the discussion by asking, **What have these activities of the past few days had in common?**

List the activities involving graphs (*How Far Did You Go?, Another Trip,* and *Warming Up*), and ask what they have had in common. Identify these all as accumulation problems and the graphs as **accumulation graphs.** Each graph shows the rate at which some quantity is gradually growing, or accumulating. In each case, the accumulation can be found as the area under the corresponding **rate graph.** (*Note: Building the Pyramid* also involved accumulation, but gave no explicit information about a rate of growth. Students will determine a rate of growth for that situation in *Filling the Reservoir* and apply the ideas discussed here at that time.)

Bring out that in each case, students found the "accumulated amount" based on the *rate* at which the accumulation was happening. You might specifically ask, **What is being "accumulated" in each of these problems?** (For the travel problems, it is distance; for the solar-collector problem, it is energy.)

You may want to mention that the study of accumulation is part of calculus. Basic calculus consists of two related components: *accumulation* (which involves the concept usually called *integration*) and *rates of change,* which students have already studied in the context of working with derivatives and will reexamine beginning with *Let It Fall.*

Looking Back at How Far Did You Go?

Have students return to their information from *How Far Did You Go?* and make a graph showing how the distance traveled increased as a function of time. (In that activity, students found only the total distance traveled.) This new graph may require a different vertical scale from the original (or a taller graph), but students can use the same horizontal scale as before.

To assist in this process, you might suggest students begin with a table of times, perhaps every 15 minutes, and find the total distance as of each time. Here are values for such a table:

Time	Distance
12:00	0
12:15	5.0
12:30	10.0
12:45	15.0
1:00	20.0
1:15	25.625
1:30	32.5
1:45	40.625
2:00	50.0
2:15	50.0
2:30	50.0
2:45	52.5
3:00	55.0
3:15	57.5
3:30	61.25
3:45	67.5
4:00	76.25
4:15	87.5
4:30	100.0
4:45	112.5
5:00	125.0

The graph of this information will look something like this:

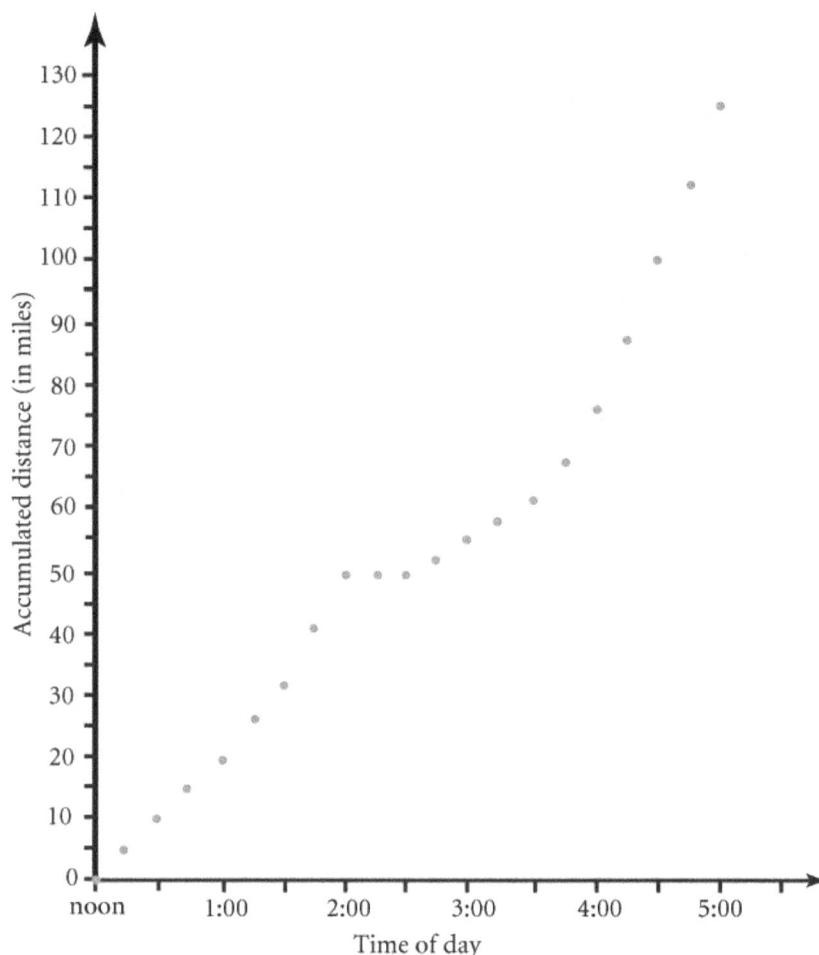

Ask, **Why isn't the distance graph linear everywhere?** Students should be able to articulate that the graph for distance is linear only if the speed is constant. Thus, the distance graph will have some sections that are linear (for instance, from noon to 1:00, when speed was constant) and some that are nonlinear (such as from 1:00 to 2:00, when speed was changing).

To help students to focus on the key idea, ask, **How do your accumulation graphs compare with the graphs they came from?** Students should compare their accumulation graphs (this new graph and the one from *Total Heat*) with the corresponding rate graphs (the graph given in *How Far Did You Go?* and the graph created through the activity *Warming Up*).

They might note these things:

- The accumulation graphs are increasing. That is, the total amount of distance traveled or energy absorbed is increasing over time.
- The rate at which the accumulation graphs increase depends on the "height" of the corresponding rate graph. Specifically, when the initial rate (speed or power) is greater, the accumulation graph is steeper.

The idea that the rate graph is the derivative of the accumulation graph should emerge gradually (though students may volunteer this idea, which is fine). The concept of derivative will be reviewed through *Let It Fall* and then applied to the accumulation context when students have a second look at *A Distance Graph* following the discussion of *Down the Drain.*

Key Questions

Does this graph look like anything you know?
What have these activities of the past few days had in common?
What is being "accumulated" in each of these problems?
Why isn't the distance graph linear everywhere?
How do your accumulation graphs compare with the graphs they came from?

Rate and Accumulation

Intent

In these activities, students use derivatives to connect the concepts of rate of growth and amount of accumulation.

Mathematics

These activities remind students that the **derivative** represents an instantaneous rate of change. Students develop the derivatives for simple power functions and encounter the **antiderivative.** They see that the accumulation function can be viewed as an antiderivative of the rate function, and the rate function as a derivative of the accumulation function. Exploration of these relationships leads to a statement of the **fundamental theorem of calculus.**

Progression

In *How Fast Were You Going?*, students use information from an accumulation graph to produce a rate graph, observing that constant speed is the slope of the distance function. *A Distance Graph* illustrates similarly that **instantaneous speed** is the derivative of the distance function, which is then reinforced in *Let It Fall!*

The next several activities establish several fundamental rules for finding derivatives. Students find the derivatives of simple power functions in *Basic Derivatives*. *Summer Job* looks at the derivative of a constant function and introduces the antiderivative. Students explore the derivative of a sum in *Going Up?* and obtain further practice in finding derivatives and antiderivatives in *Polynomial Derivatives*.

Zero to Sixty and *Area and Distance* help students to clarify the relationships among speed, distance, and acceleration in terms of derivatives and antiderivatives. Along with *A Fundamental Relationship*, this introduces the fundamental theorem of calculus. Finally, students explore growth rates of areas and volumes for some simple geometric figures in *The Leading Edge,* preparing them to move directly to a solution of the pyramid unit problem.

How Fast Were You Going?
A Distance Graph
Let It Fall!
Basic Derivatives
Summer Job
Going Up?
Down the Drain
Zero to Sixty

Polynomial Derivatives
Area and Distance
A Fundamental Relationship
The Leading Edge

How Fast Were You Going?

Intent

Students use an accumulation graph to construct a rate graph.

Mathematics

Students now consider the reverse of the accumulation process that was the focus of the discussion following *Total Heat*. In that discussion, students used a graph of a rate (power or speed) to make a graph of the accumulated amount (energy or distance). Now they will start with an accumulation graph—in this case, distance traveled—and graph the rate (speed).

Progression

Students make a speed graph, which gives a rate, from a distance graph, which represents accumulation. The subsequent discussion points out that they can use "rise over run" triangles to estimate speeds and thus that slopes on the cumulative distance graph represent speeds.

Although students might recognize that the rate graph function is the derivative of the accumulation graph function, this understanding is not expected until after they examine the concept of derivative in connection with *Let It Fall!* and calculate a derivative using algebra. They will then develop the general principle that the function for an accumulation graph can be found by looking for a function whose derivative is the rate graph. That is, the accumulation function is the antiderivative of the rate function (or, as students will see, *an* antiderivative of the rate function).

This principle, which is the essence of the fundamental theorem of calculus, is stated in the discussion following *Down the Drain*. At that point, students will digress for more algebraic work to see that finding derivatives (and hence antiderivatives) can be, at least in some cases, a fairly straightforward algebraic process.

Approximate Time

25 minutes for activity (at home or in class)
15 to 20 minutes for discussion

Classroom Organization

Individuals, followed by whole-class discussion

Doing the Activity

No introduction to this activity is necessary.

Discussing and Debriefing the Activity

For Question 1, if students do complex computations and overlook the obvious, help them see that the total trip was 45 miles and took 1 hour, so the average speed was simply 45 mph.

For Question 2, students will probably have recognized that a linear portion of the graph for the distance traveled implies a constant rate of speed; this principle can be brought out explicitly through Question 3. (In earlier activities, students saw this principle in reverse, namely, that a constant speed implies a linear change in distance.)

The graph indicates a constant speed for each of three time periods (noon to 12:20, 12:20 to 12:50, and 12:50 to 1:00). To get the speed for each time interval (respectively, 30 mph, 60 mph, and 30 mph), students divide the distance traveled during the interval by the length of the time interval.

It's worthwhile making this process explicit, perhaps having students draw "rise over run" triangles on the graph. Emphasize that for each segment, they could pick any pair of points for calculating the average speed and get the same result.

As a part of this discussion, try to elicit the idea that the speed is itself a new function, "derived" from the distance function. The word *derived* is used here as a hint to the concept of *derivative.*

To bring out the behavior at transition points of the graph, ask, What happens at 12:20? The car seems to change speed instantaneously from 30 miles per hour to 60 miles per hour. Help students see that as this is physically impossible—the car has to transition from one speed to another—showing the graph as a set of line segments is a bit unrealistic. An actual distance graph cannot suddenly shift from a line with one slope to a line with another slope, and an actual speed graph cannot suddenly jump from one horizontal segment to another. This feature of step functions also arose in the discussion of *What's Watt?*

You might have students look back at the graph from *How Far Did You Go?* In that activity, students treated the steep segments as if they were vertical when, in fact, they could not be vertical (as the car couldn't move without the passage of time).

Speed Is Slope

Help students connect the speeds they found to the slopes of the line segments. Focus on one segment and ask, What would you call the value you found for the speed if you just had the graph without the context? Students should see that, in dividing the distance by the time, they are simply calculating the standard difference quotient for slope.

Thus, the graph has an associated "slope graph" in which, for a given horizontal coordinate, the corresponding vertical coordinate is the slope of the initial graph at that horizontal coordinate. You might refer to this as the "slope graph" in anticipation of the idea of the graph of the derivative.

You might then ask, **Can you average the speeds for the three time intervals (30, 60, and 30) to get the overall average?** Help students see that this doesn't work because they need to take into account the amount of time traveled at each speed.

From Speed Back to Distance

Next, ask students to use their graph of the speed function (which should be a step function with three horizontal segments) to create a graph of the distance traveled. (If they immediately realize that this gets them back to the original distance graph, they don't necessarily have to go through the process.)

Use this connection to reinforce the general principle. **In general, how are the rate graph and the accumulation graph related?** (This idea was addressed in part at the end of the discussion of *Total Heat.*)

You might emphasize the simple case here in which the rate graph is a step function and thus the accumulation graph is a sequence of (usually nonhorizontal) line segments.

Students might now state that the rate graph comes from finding the slope of the distance graph and the distance graph comes from finding the area under the rate graph. It is important they see the reciprocal relationship here: either graph can be used to create the other.

Does the relationship between the speed and distance graphs share a similarity with a relationship in the solar energy problem? Students should see that "rate of energy absorption" is like speed and that "accumulated energy" is like distance, so the same reciprocal relationship exists in this context as well.

Key Questions

What happens at 12:20?
What would you call the value you found for the speed if you just had the graph without the context?
In general, how are the rate graph and the accumulation graph related?
Does the relationship between the speed and distance graphs share a similarity with a relationship in the solar problem?

A Distance Graph

Intent

Students construct a speed graph from a distance graph that exhibits gradual acceleration.

Mathematics

This activity is similar to *How Fast Were You Going?*, but involving a curved distance graph.

Progression

Given a curved graph of distance traveled as a function of time, students find the average speed for the entire time graphed, estimate the speed at a number of points in time, and graph speed as a function of time.

Students will reexamine this activity following the discussion of *Down the Drain*, when they will generalize from *slope* to *derivative*. Students need to save their results from this activity for comparison at that time.

Approximate Time

35 to 40 minutes

Classroom Organization

Small groups or individuals, followed by whole-class discussion

Doing the Activity

You might begin by asking students to compare the graph in this activity with the one in *How Fast Were You Going?* Help them see that because this graph is curved, rather than a sequence of line segments, it represents a more realistic situation. On the other hand, a curved graph will make the process of creating the speed graph considerably more difficult.

Point out that the vertical scale for the new graph will represent "feet per second" instead of "feet."

Discussing and Debriefing the Activity

Although Question 1 may seem elementary, it's probably worthwhile reviewing. The car traveled 800 feet in 20 seconds, for an average speed of 40 feet per second.

For Question 2, have students carefully describe their process for finding the speeds. Getting accurate data requires them to be very careful. Some students may recognize that what they want at each value of t is the slope for the approximating straight line (that is, the tangent line), but it is not essential that this be articulated now.

Students' estimates of the rates are likely to vary. Be on the alert for interesting variations in technique. For instance, students might use the segment connecting the points for $t = 9$ and $t = 11$ to get the speed for $t = 10$. Because the graph is quadratic, this actually gives the correct value, but this technique would not give exact values for every graph.

As students put their "speed values" together in Question 3, you might once again emphasize that they are graphing a new function that is derived from the original function by a process of estimating slopes. They might see that this "slope graph" is approximately linear, but this recognition is not essential.

Save the results from this activity for comparison based on insights from calculus in the discussion of *Down the Drain*.

Let It Fall!

Intent

Students recognize the derivative as instantaneous speed and as the limit of a secant slope.

Mathematics

This activity reviews the fundamental idea of a **derivative** in the context of a real-world situation, emphasizing that the derivative is, in a sense, an average rate of change taken over a very short time interval.

Progression

Students estimate the instantaneous speed of a freely falling object by finding its average speed over increasingly smaller intervals. The subsequent discussion reminds them that an instantaneous rate of change is also known as a derivative. It emphasizes that the derivative is itself a function. The class then uses similar reasoning to develop an algebraic form to calculate the derivate of the function $d(t) = 16t^2$.

Approximate Time

30 minutes for activity (at home or in class)
25 minutes for discussion

Classroom Organization

Individuals, followed by whole-class discussion

Doing the Activity

No introduction to this activity is needed.

Discussing and Debriefing the Activity

Questions 1 and 2

Although going over the details of these questions may be unnecessary for some students, it can provide a solid foundation for the concept of **instantaneous speed,** so it's probably wise to review at least Question 1. If necessary, have students articulate once again that the average speed for any time interval is the distance traveled during the interval divided by elapsed time.

IMP Year 4, *How Much? How Fast?* Unit, Teacher's Guide

© 2012 Interactive Mathematics Program

42

Students will likely answer Question 1f by noting a trend in the average speeds as the interval gets smaller. Thus

- From $t = 3$ to $t = 5$ (Question 1b), the average speed is 128 feet per second.
- From $t = 4$ to $t = 5$ (Question 1c), the average speed is 144 feet per second.
- From $t = 4.9$ to $t = 5$ (Question 1d), the average speed is 158.4 feet per second.
- From $t = 4.99$ to $t = 5$ (Question 1e), the average speed is 159.84 feet per second.

From these values, students will likely estimate that the speed at the instant of impact is 160 feet per second. If needed, have them look at even smaller time intervals.

Similarly, for Question 2d, they should find that the instantaneous speed at $t = 2$ is 64 feet per second.

Question 3: A Table of Instantaneous Speeds

For Question 3, have students share the instantaneous speeds they found for other values of t, and put these values into a table such as this one:

t (seconds)	Instantaneous speed (feet per second)
1	32
2	64
3	96
4	128
5	160

Then ask, Is there an instantaneous speed at each moment? Could we calculate it? The affirmative answer means there is a function whose value at $t = a$ is the instantaneous speed at which the bundle is falling a seconds after being dropped. Based on the table, students will probably see that this function seems to be defined by the expression $32a$.

An Instantaneous Rate Is a Derivative

If it hasn't yet come up, ask, What is another name for this instantaneous rate? As needed, remind students that this is called a **derivative.**

Sketch a graph of the bundle's height as a function of time, and ask, **What does the derivative for a given value of t say about the graph?** As needed, remind students that the derivative for a particular value of t is the slope of the line tangent to the graph at that point. For instance, the value 96 in the table is the slope of the line tangent to the height graph at the point (3, 144). The second coordinate comes from the fact that $d(3) = 16 \cdot 3^2$.

This is a good opportunity to introduce or review the notation for derivatives. For example, ask, **How do we write the fact that the derivative of the function d has the value 96 when $t = 3$?** Establish that this is written $d'(3) = 96$. [*Note:* Throughout this unit, we denote the derivative of a function $y = f(x)$ as y' or $f'(x)$ rather than the more common but potentially confusing $\dfrac{dy}{dx}$. The latter notation is more useful in some contexts but would not be especially helpful here.]

The Derivative Is a Function

Be sure students recognize that the values of the derivative for different points form a function—namely, the function describing the table just created. You might have them plot the points in the table and see that they are on the graph of the linear function $s = 32t$, where s represents speed, and then use the graph or equation to obtain the speed for a value that is not in the table, such as $t = 2.75$.

This may be a good time to combine derivative notation with the idea of a derivative as a function. If $d'(3) = 96$ and $d'(5) = 160$, then in general $d'(t) = 32t$. Compare this formulation with $d(t) = 16t^2$ to reinforce the notions that both are functions and that the prime notation is used to distinguish the two.

The Derivative Using Algebra

The next challenge is for students to show, using algebra, that the rule they found for the table is correct.

Ask, **What is an expression for the bundle's average speed over an arbitrary time interval?** It's helpful to use a letter other than t to represent the instant at which the instantaneous rate is being found (such as a, used in the preceding discussion) and another (traditionally h) to represent the duration of the time interval under consideration.

Students will probably represent the average speed by either $\dfrac{d(a) - d(a - h)}{h}$ or $\dfrac{d(a + h) - d(a)}{h}$, where $d(t) = 16t^2$ is the function given in the activity for the distance the bundle falls in t seconds. The first expression gives the average speed during the h seconds leading up to $t = a$. The second gives the average speed for the h seconds right after $t = a$. The first expression is probably like what students did in Question 1, which involved intervals *up to* a given moment, while they may have used both expressions in Question 2.

Have students replace the expression $d(x)$ by the full expression for the function. Thus, the first expression becomes $\dfrac{16a^2 - 16(a-h)^2}{h}$. They should be able to expand and simplify the numerator to $32ah - 16h^2$ and simplify the resulting fraction to $32a - 16h$. Similarly, the second expression simplifies to $32a + 16h$. You might point out that $32a - 16h$ is the same as $32a + 16h$ except with $-h$ in place of h. (*Note:* This algebraic manipulation might be challenging for some students on their own; it's fine if they simply follow along as others work through the details.)

Now ask, **For a given value of *a*, what happens as *h* gets smaller?** Students should see that, whichever expression they use, they get simply $32a$, which is the rule they found from their table. Have them verify again that this is consistent with the results for Questions 2 and 3 for particular values of *a*.

Derivatives in the Abstract

Bring out that this computational process can be used in any context or even when there is no context. For a function $y = f(x)$, the derivative of this function at $x = a$, written $f'(a)$, is the value approached by the ratio

$$\frac{f(a+h)-f(a)}{h}$$

as *h* gets smaller and smaller.

In particular, students have just proved that for the function $d(t) = 16t^2$, the derivative at any fixed value a is $d'(a) = 32a$. Because this is true for every possible value of the variable (that is, for any $t = a$), they have defined the *derivative function* in this case: $d'(t) = 32t$.

Ask, **What do the numerator *d*(*a* + *h*) − *d*(*a*) and the denominator *h* mean in the context of the problem?** The numerator is the distance the bundle falls in the time interval from $t = a$ to $t = a + h$, while *h* represents the length of this time interval. Thus, the ratio $\dfrac{d(a+h)-d(a)}{h}$ has the form "distance/time" and represents the average speed during the time interval.

You can connect the derivative ratio $\dfrac{f(a+h)-f(a)}{h}$ with slope using a diagram like the one here, which also appears in the student book in *Basic Derivatives*. Students should recognize the numerator, $f(a + h) - f(a)$, as the "rise" and the denominator, *h*, as the "run." Be sure they see that *h* is the same as $(a + h) - a$.

Ask, **What line does this ratio relate to?** Students should be able to identify the ratio as the slope of the secant line connecting $(a, f(a))$ to $(a + h, f(a + h))$, and see that this is close to the slope of the line tangent to the curve at $(a, f(a))$.

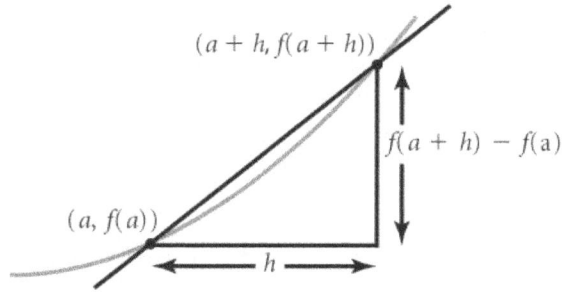

Key Questions

Is there an instantaneous speed at each moment? Could we calculate it?
What is another name for this instantaneous rate?
If we look at a graph of the bundle's height as a function of time, what does the derivative for a given value of t say about the graph?
For a given value of a, what happens as h gets smaller?

Basic Derivatives

Intent

Students find the derivatives for some simple power functions.

Mathematics

Students discover that they can use algebra to find derivatives of power functions without a lot of work (at least for small exponents).

Progression

For each of five power functions, students use the definition of a **derivative** to calculate the derivate at four points, look for a pattern, develop a general rule for the derivative of the function, and then justify that rule using algebra. In the subsequent discussion, the class begins a poster of derivative rules, develops a general rule for differentiating $f(x) = x^n$, and establishes that multiplying a function by a constant multiplies its derivative by that constant.

Students will use the results from this activity in the discussion of *Summer Job*. *Summer Job* can be assigned as homework before *Basic Derivatives* has been discussed, but the discussion of *Basic Derivatives* should precede the discussion of *Summer Job*.

Approximate Time

25 to 30 minutes for activity (considerably more time will be required if students work individually rather than in groups)
15 minutes for discussion

Classroom Organization

Small groups, followed by whole-class discussion

Doing the Activity

For each of the first four functions, have students assign one of the numeric calculations to each group member and then create a group table to look for a pattern. All students should then try to do the general calculation using a variable. This will give everyone some practice but get them through the four cases fairly quickly.

Discussing and Debriefing the Activity

As students present their results for the derivatives, encourage them occasionally to return to the meaning of derivative as the slope of an approximating line and to explain the geometric meaning of the numerator and denominator of their ratios.

For Questions 2 and 3, insist that students start each problem using a point-by-point method. That is, they should display derivatives for specific values of x before moving to the algebraic approach. For instance, on Question 2 [$g(x) = x^3$], they might develop a table like this to begin with, including enough values to find a pattern. If they have trouble finding a rule for this table, you might suggest they examine the values for $\dfrac{g'(x)}{3}$, and similarly for Question 3.

x	$g'(x)$
1	3
2	12
3	27
4	48
5	75

Now is a good time to begin posting a list of rules, or principles, for derivatives. You may want to post the results from Questions 1 to 3 for subsequent reference, and ask students if they see a pattern. If so, have them articulate that pattern and confirm whether it is correct.

Multiplying by a Constant

One simple general principle is that if you multiply a differentiable function $f(x)$ by a constant, say a, the derivative of the product $a \cdot f(x)$ is simply a times the derivative $f'(x)$. Questions 4 and 5 develop this principle.

For Question 4, be sure students see that the derivative is the same for each x-value because the graph is a straight line and, therefore, its slope isn't changing. Elicit the idea that, for a linear function, the derivative is the same thing as the slope.

You might also have students compare the graphs of $y = 5x$ and $y = x$ to see that the rate of change of one is 5 times that of the other and, therefore, its derivative should be 5 times as great.

Question 5 begins to generalize this relationship by examining a constant multiple of another simple function whose derivative is already known. Here are three ways

IMP Year 4, *How Much? How Fast?* Unit, Teacher's Guide

© 2012 Interactive Mathematics Program

48

to examine the idea that the derivative of the function $y = 5x^2$ is 5 times the derivative of $y = x^2$:

- By finding derivatives for specific points: This will allow students to see the pattern that the derivatives are 5 times as large.
- By algebraic analysis: Students might go through the steps used for earlier examples and see that the factor of 5 carries through to the end of the computation.
- By a heuristic argument: For instance, if two areas are both increasing, and one is always 5 times the other, then as the smaller one grows, the larger one must grow 5 times as fast to maintain the ratio of the areas.

Have students generalize their results from Questions 4 and 5 and add them to the poster of derivative rules.

Supplemental Activity

Derivative Power **(extension)** explores the question of finding the derivative of $f(x) = x^n$ analytically.

Summer Job

Intent

Students develop a rule for the derivative of a constant function.

Mathematics

A general principle of calculus is that if you start with one function and add a constant to get a second function (that is, if the numeric difference between the functions is a constant), the two functions have the same derivative. A related principle is that the derivative of a constant function (or a constant term) is zero. This activity uses two parallel functions to develop this idea. The class discussion will introduce the term **antiderivative** and bring out the fact that a given function has many antiderivatives.

Progression

Students consider the context of two people who are earning the same wages and saving at the same rate, but start with differing account balances. They write equations for the account balances as a function of hours worked, graph the equations, find and graph the derivatives of those functions, and describe the relationships among the various graphs.

The subsequent discussion establishes that adding a constant to a function does not change its derivative. It also introduces the concept of an antiderivative and establishes that every function has infinitely many antiderivatives. Finally, it brings out that an accumulation function determines the corresponding rate function, but not the converse.

Approximate Time

30 minutes for activity (at home or in class)
20 minutes for discussion

Classroom Organization

Individuals, followed by whole-class discussion

Doing the Activity

This activity requires no introduction.

Discussing and Debriefing the Activity

Students' graphs for Question 2 should be parallel lines, so their two graphs for Question 4 should be the same horizontal line, representing a savings rate of $5.70 per hour. Insist they use proper units to label the axes and describe the quantities.

The discussion of Question 5 should bring out these points:

- Parallel lines mean equal slopes or rates of change and thus equal derivatives.
- Straight lines mean constant slopes and thus constant (horizontal) derivative functions.
- Constant derivative functions mean that the original functions that generated them must be straight lines.

Now ask students to consider the two equations describing the functions in Question 1 and ask, How might you calculate their derivatives algebraically? They will probably suggest differentiating each expression term by term, and you can confirm that this is correct. (*Going Up?* establishes the more general principle that the derivative of a sum of two functions is the sum of their derivatives.) This procedure quickly leads to the conclusion that the derivative of each constant term is zero.

Since derivatives measure rates of change of functions, the notion of the derivative of a number doesn't make sense. You might have students think about a constant function, say an oven temperature that stays at 350° for 30 minutes. Ask them to construct an equation for the situation and explain why its derivative is zero.

If additional justification is warranted, have students use the slope ratio from the discussion following *Let It Fall!* to calculate the derivative of $J(h) = 5.7h + 280$. They should see that the constant term simply subtracts out and disappears.

The Antiderivative

To develop the idea of an **antiderivative,** return to the language of rate and accumulation functions. What processes are occurring as you move from the function $J(h)$ to the function $J'(h)$? Students should note measuring a rate of change, finding a slope, and taking a derivative. Point out that it is often useful to move the other direction, from a rate function to an associated accumulation function. In fact, this is precisely what the two unit problems—pyramid volume and solar energy collection—require. Explain that this reverse process is called, appropriately, *antidifferentiation,* or finding an *antiderivative*.

For example, begin with the function $f(x) = 2x$. Is $g(x) = x^2$ an antiderivative of $f(x)$? If so, why? Make sure students see that finding an antiderivative involves identifying another function whose derivative is the first function.

Encourage students to use this reasoning to find antiderivatives for $r(x) = 4x^3$ and $s(x) = 10x$ (from Questions 3 and 5 of *Basic Derivatives*). They will probably come up with something like $h(x) = x^4$ and $p(x) = 5x^2$. (Unfortunately, there is no simple standard notation for antiderivatives. If the functional notation seems confusing, students can just work with the expressions, keeping in mind that they represent functions. Thus it's okay to say that x^4 is an antiderivative of $4x^3$.)

If someone proposes, say, $h(x) = x^4 + 1$, insist on a justification that this is also correct. This example could lead to the next idea.

Many Antiderivatives

Now you can return to the functions in *Summer Job*. Is $J(h) = 5.7h + 280$ an antiderivative of the function $f(h) = 5.7$? If so, why? Repeat the question for Rex's equation. Is $R(h) = 5.7h + 350$ an antiderivative of the function $f(h) = 5.7$? Why?

Then pose the teaser, What is *the* antiderivative of $f(h) = 5.7$? The answer, of course, is that f has not just one antiderivative, but an infinite number, all of the form $g(h) = 5.7h + k$, where k is any numeric constant.

Reinforce this idea with a few more examples, perhaps having students generate various antiderivatives for $4x^3$ and $10x$. You might also use a pair of "parallel" curves, such as shown here, to illustrate the principle more generally.

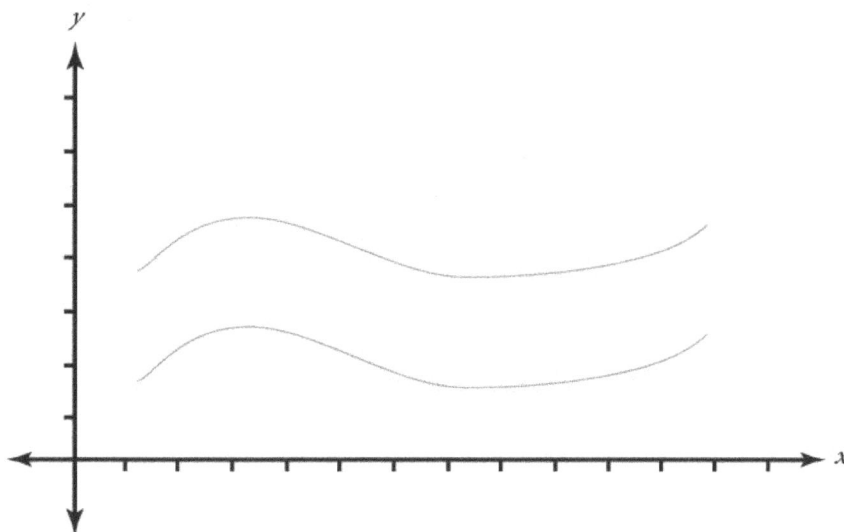

Get students to articulate this principle in its broadest form. One way to express it is, "If $g(x)$ is an antiderivative of $f(x)$, then $g(x) + k$ is also an antiderivative for any constant value k." Encourage various expressions of the idea. Emphasize that this means one should talk about *an* antiderivative of a given function rather than *the* antiderivative.

As a final point, use *Summer Job* as an example of accumulation and rate functions. First examine the direction posed in the activity: If you are given an accumulation function, can you determine its corresponding rate function? After students have affirmed this, challenge them with the opposite question: If you are given a rate function, can you determine its accumulation function? Appropriate answers would be something like "not completely" or "up to a constant increment."

Encourage students to state these relationships clearly, in general terms. A more intuitive formulation of the second direction is that even if we know how fast something is growing, we also need to know how big it was "at the start" to determine its size as a function of time. This principle is behind students' earlier work with linear functions, for which they have seen they need both a rate and a "starting value" to determine the function. (Actually, any given value will do, though the initial value is most common.)

Conclude the activity by having students add the new rules or principles they have discovered to the class poster.

Key Questions

Is $J(h) = 5.7h + 280$ an antiderivative of the function $f(h) = 5.7$? Why?
Is $R(h) = 5.7h + 350$ an antiderivative of the function $f(h) = 5.7$? Why?
What is *the* antiderivative of $f(h) = 5.7$?
If you are given an accumulation function, can you determine its corresponding rate function?
If you are given a rate function, can you determine its accumulation function?

Going Up?

Intent

Students explore the derivative of a sum of two functions.

Mathematics

This activity uses two similar contexts to suggest that the derivative of a sum is the sum of the derivatives.

Progression

Students examine two situations: a person walking up an escalator and walking on a moving train. In each case, they use the graphs of two functions to sketch the graph of the sum of the functions. They then consider how the graphs are related and how the various speeds are related. The subsequent discussion establishes that the derivative of a sum of two functions is the sum of the derivatives.

Approximate Time

30 minutes for activity (at home or in class)
10 minutes for discussion

Classroom Organization

Individuals, followed by whole-class discussion

Doing the Activity

This activity requires no introduction.

Discussing and Debriefing the Activity

Question 1

For parts a and b, students should be able to articulate that the slope of each graph gives the speed. Both graphs start at (0, 0), so the point (5, 10) for f shows that the escalator is rising 2 feet per second, and the point (5, 15) for g shows that Gabriel climbs the steps at 3 feet per second.

For part c, students might use their previous answers to see that the graph should be based on the equation $h = 5t$, by adding the speeds. If so, ask, How might you get the graph for *k* directly from the two graphs, rather than by using the speeds? As needed, lead the class through the point-by-point addition process:

- Pick a value for *t.*
- Find the *h*-value for that value of *t* for each function.
- Add the two *h*-values.
- Use the sum as the *h*-value for the function *k.*

Identify the function *k* as the *sum of f and g.*

For part d, students should articulate that the speed at which Gabriel rises when he is climbing the moving stairs is the sum of the two speeds.

How are the slopes of the three lines related? This question will both review the connection between speed and slope and lay the groundwork for the more general idea about the derivative of the sum of two functions. You might be able to get students to articulate a general principle that when two linear functions are added, the slope of the sum is the sum of the two slopes.

Question 2

To prepare for the general principle, ask students for the slope of the line (the function *g*), so they see it is the same as Gabriel's walking speed (2 feet per second, different from his climbing speed in Question 1).

For part b, students probably estimated from the curve. Have volunteers explain how they did this. For instance, to find $f'(4)$, they might have drawn a line tangent to the curve and seen that it went approximately through the points (2, 0) and (8, 12), for a slope of about 2. Thus, after 4 seconds, the train is going about 2 feet per second. Other students might use different pairs of points to estimate this slope. Be sure students recognize that they are simply making estimates.

You might point out that $f'(4)$ is roughly the same as the slope of *g,* and ask about the significance of this fact. Students should see that the tangent line is roughly parallel to the graph of *g.*

For $f'(6)$, the tangent line goes approximately through (4, 2) and (8, 17), for a slope of about 3.75. So, after 6 seconds, the train is traveling about 3.75 feet per second.

Because students don't have a formula for the nonlinear function *f,* they will have to find the graph of *k* by a point-by-point approach. They might do this numerically, by estimating the *d*-values and adding them [for instance, $f(4) \approx 4$ and $g(4) \approx 8$, so $k(4) \approx 12$], or geometrically, by "adding" the vertical segments up from the *t*-axis to each graph. The next diagram shows the points on the new graph that have *t*-coordinates that are integers.

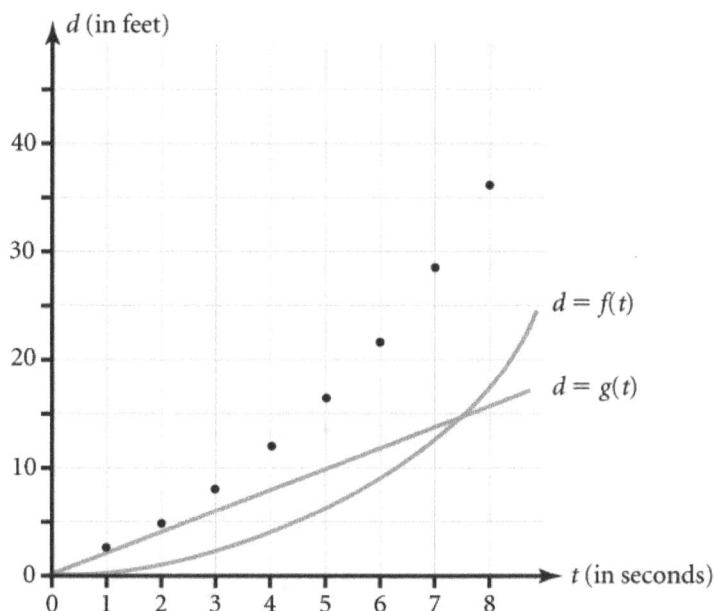

The tangent line to the new graph, at $t = 4$, goes roughly through the points (2, 3) and (8, 28), for a slope of a little more than 4, which is approximately the sum of the slope of g and the value $f'(4)$.

Similarly, students might find that the tangent line to the new graph, at $t = 6$, goes roughly through the points (3, 5) and (8, 34), for a slope of about 5.8, which is roughly the sum of the slope of g and the value $f'(6)$.

Summarizing the Principle

Out of this discussion should emerge the natural principle that if two functions are added, then for each t-value, the derivative of the sum function at that t-value is the sum of the derivatives of the two functions at that t-value. Or simply, "the derivative of a sum is the sum of the derivatives."

Add this principle to the class poster of derivative rules.

Key Questions

How might you get the graph for k directly from the two graphs, rather than by using the speeds?
How are the slopes of the three lines related?

Down the Drain

Intent

Students look at the graphical representation of negative rate and accumulation.

Mathematics

This activity involves the analysis of a decreasing function and its derivative.

Progression

Students are guided through the analysis of a draining bathtub as an example of negative rate and accumulation. They graph a function for the amount of water in the tub as a function of time, as well as the derivative function. Following the discussion of this activity, they revisit *A Distance Graph* in terms of derivatives. They apply the derivative as instantaneous speed and as the slope of a line tangent to the curve.

Approximate Time

25 to 30 minutes for activity (at home or in class)
15 to 20 minutes for discussion

Classroom Organization

Individuals, followed by whole-class discussion

Doing the Activity

Introduce this activity as another example of rate and accumulation, but with a twist. Questions 1 to 3 ought to be fairly routine by now.

For Question 4, some students might be confused about the "accumulation" function, since in this case it is a depletion function. You might just remind them that accumulation measures the amount (how much) of the dependent quantity.

If students aren't sure how to approach Question 5a, you might ask, What is the rate at $t = 1$ second? How much water is in the tub at that time? This should alert them to the fact that they need to know how much water was in the tub at the start (knowing the amount at any other time would also suffice).

Question 5b gets at the point of this activity, which is interpreting area under a curve as "negative area" if the curve lies below the x-axis.

Discussing and Debriefing the Activity

Questions 1 and 2 are straightforward. As students present their answers to Question 3, have them interpret the equation and graph, explaining the meaning of the negative values.

Mechanically, Question 4 involves nothing more than calculating the slope. Again, students should explain the significance of the negative rate. Discuss the fact that normally the word *accumulation* implies an increase in some quantity, such as wealth or mold. As used here, the word is more neutral, meaning "amount." If the amount in question is decreasing, it can be described as a negative accumulation. An analogy might be *growth,* as in the growth of the economy; usually this is positive, but a recession involves "negative growth."

The most likely response to Question 5a is "the amount of water in the tub when the drain is opened." It might be helpful to identify this information as representing a particular point on the accumulation graph, namely (0, 224). Help students generalize this notion to "the starting value" and relate it to similar problems they've seen in other units.

If someone suggests using instead the time when the water runs out, have the student explain how to work backward from that value to reconstruct the amount of water at prior values of *t*. Point out that again we have to rely on knowing a particular point, in this case (280, 0).

Students may have various explanations for Question 5b. If no one takes the approach of measuring the area "under" the rate graph, ask, How could you use the idea of the area under the rate graph to measure accumulation? The key idea is that a given point on the rate graph, say (20, –0.8), represents a positive time and a negative rate, so their product represents a negative amount. This conforms to previous interpretations of "the area under the graph" if this concept is broadened to "the area bounded by the graph and the *x*-axis" and any areas below the axis are considered negative. Given this interpretation, the change in amount over any given time interval can be measured directly, and this coupled with the initial value can be used to construct the accumulation graph.

The concept of negative area will not appear in any further activities in *How Much? How Fast?* but it is a powerful idea that is used extensively in calculus theory and applications.

Revisit "A Distance Graph"

Summer Job and *Down the Drain* explored derivatives and antiderivatives as rates and accumulations using equations in linear contexts. *A Distance Graph* and *Going Up?* involved nonlinear contexts but used approximate values measured from a graph. In the next few activities, students will combine these approaches to get exact values in nonlinear situations.

In *A Distance Graph*, students used the graph to estimate instantaneous speeds at various times. Have them review that activity briefly, recalling what they did and retrieving their data table and graph for speed. You might ask them to apply the language they've developed about derivatives and tangent lines to that activity.

Ask whether students recognize the shape of the distance graph. They may conjecture that it is a parabola, and you can confirm this as well as reveal that its equation is $s = 2t^2$. Ask, **How could you use this information to find the instantaneous speed at any time t?** By now, students should recognize this as the derivative function and be able to calculate it algebraically. Have them compare this result to the data and graph they generated in that earlier activity and verify that they match. Encourage them to use appropriate symbolic notation, such as $s'(t) = 4t$ and $s'(10) = 40$, and to state in words what these expressions and equations mean.

An important point to bring out is that the speeds students found and plotted were *instantaneous* speeds—that is, derivatives—and that these speeds could also be described as the slopes of the tangent lines at the given points. For instance, if students estimated the speed at $t = 10$ to be 40 feet per second, they are saying that the tangent line at the point (10, 200) has a slope of 40 and that, at $t = 10$, the derivative of the distance function is 40.

Once again, raise the connection between rate and accumulation. Prompt students to articulate the reciprocal nature of this relationship, noting that it holds with nonlinear as well as linear functions. At this point, they should be able to state that the derivative of the distance function is the speed function and that, consequently, the speed function is an antiderivative of the distance function. They will deepen their understanding of this relationship over the next several activities.

Key Questions

What is the rate at $t = 1$ second? How much water is in the tub at that time?
How could you use the idea of the area under the rate graph to measure accumulation?

Zero to Sixty

Intent

Students interpret acceleration, speed, and distance as derivatives and antiderivatives.

Mathematics

This activity offers another model for connecting rate and accumulation.

Progression

Presented with a car that, with constant acceleration, can reach a speed of 60 miles per hour in 10 seconds, students graph speed as a function of time and find the total distance traveled during several time intervals. The subsequent discussion reminds them that they can calculate the distance using the area under the speed graph, or they can find an antiderivative of the speed function. The discussion reinforces the concept that accumulation functions are antiderivatives of the corresponding rate functions and then summarizes the derivative rules developed so far.

Approximate Time

30 minutes for activity (at home or in class)
20 minutes for discussion

Classroom Organization

Individuals, followed by whole-class discussion

Materials

Optional: Transparency of the *Zero to Sixty* blackline master

Doing the Activity

This activity requires no introduction.

Discussing and Debriefing the Activity

You might choose to omit discussion of Question 1 or simply have a brief presentation to clarify the change in units.

Acceleration

As students present their graphs for Question 2, bring out that the straight line indicates that speed is increasing at a constant rate. Get students to recall from *The Diver Returns* that a change in speed is called *acceleration*. Ask, What does the linear speed graph in this situation imply about the car's acceleration? Students should be able to conclude that acceleration is constant.

In straight-line motion, acceleration measures the rate of change of speed with respect to time, so the acceleration function is the derivative of the speed function. Have students calculate this derivative and put into words what the result means.

Speed and Distance

It will probably be useful to have a well-drawn graph for Question 2 available as students go over the details of Question 3, which is the heart of the activity. A blackline master of this graph is supplied.

For the various parts of Question 3, students might use the area principle articulated early in the unit, or they might find the average speed by averaging the initial and final speeds for each interval. For instance, the shaded area on this graph represents the distance traveled from $t = 2$ to $t = 4$ (part b).

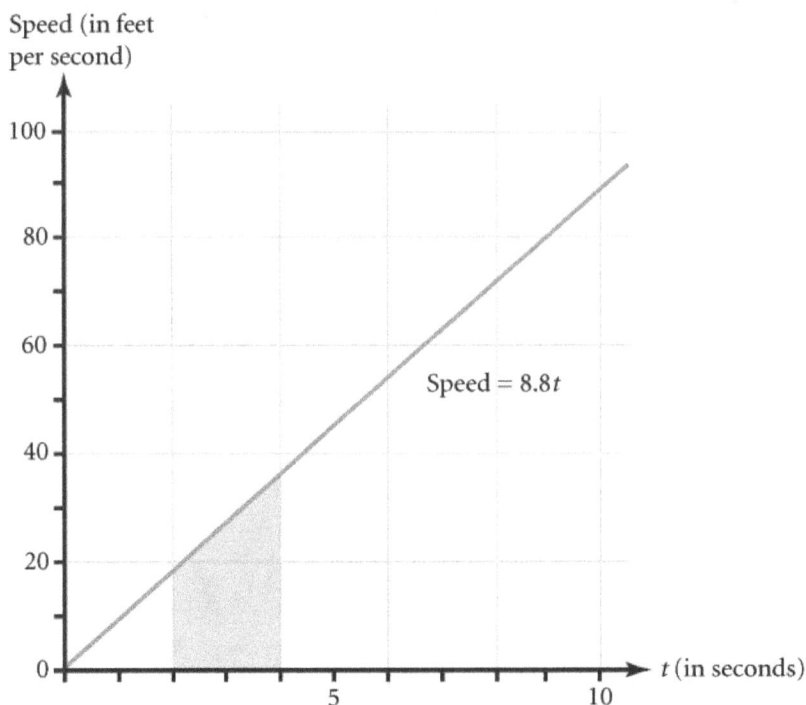

You might put the information for Question 3 in a table, including a column for the total distance so far.

Time interval	Distance (feet)	Total distance so far (feet)
$t = 0$ to $t = 2$	17.6	17.6
$t = 2$ to $t = 4$	52.8	70.4
$t = 4$ to $t = 6$	88	158.4
$t = 6$ to $t = 8$	123.2	281.6
$t = 8$ to $t = 10$	158.4	440

You may want to confirm the total distance through $t = 10$ in at least two ways:

- The final speed is 88 feet per second, so the average speed is 44 feet per second. Over a period of 10 seconds, this is 440 feet.
- The total area under the speed graph is a triangle, with base 10 (from $t = 0$ to $t = 10$) and height 88 (because at $t = 10$, the speed is 88 feet per second). So the area is $10 \cdot 88 \div 2$, or 440.

Ask, How could you use your data or the geometry of the graph to get an algebraic rule for the distance traveled as a function of t? Students should be able to use either of the two methods just described (using the average speed or finding the area) to do this.

For example, they could see that after t seconds, the car is going $8.8t$ feet per second, so its average has been $4.4t$ feet per second. Traveling at this average speed for t seconds produces a distance given by the equation $d(t) = 4.4t^2$ feet. (The area analysis is similar.) You might have students confirm this formula by comparison with the last column of the table. For instance, substituting $t = 6$ gives 158.4.

When students have constructed a data table and an equation, have them sketch the graph of the distance function.

The Derivative of the Distance Function

Now focus on the main idea. What is the derivative of this function? Students should be able to calculate $d'(t) = 8.8t$ and state that this is the same as the speed function $s(t)$.

One basic aspect of this relationship is that "of course" the derivative of the distance function must be the speed function. After all, speed is the derivative of distance, because speed measures the rate at which the object's position (distance from the start) is changing.

Viewed in the other direction, the distance function is an antiderivative of the speed function. Clarify that this means students could have found the distance function without performing any of the step-by-step computations they did in the activity. That is, they could simply find an appropriate antiderivative for the function $s(t) = 8.8t$, which they can now compute based on their work in *Basic Derivatives* and *Summer Job*.

This might be a good time to post a general principle such as the following:

> **If you start with a function and get a corresponding accumulation function, then if you take the derivative of that new function, you get back to the original function.**

In other words, if $y = f(t)$ is the original function and $y = F(t)$ is its accumulation function, then $F'(t) = f(t)$. The function f is the derivative of F, and the function F is an antiderivative of f.

Point out that the conclusion just reached about the activity is an application of this general principle, because the distance function from the activity is an accumulation function for the speed function.

The original function f does not even have to represent a rate; the abstract power functions in *Basic Derivatives* are examples. The accumulation can simply be the accumulated area between the curve and the x-axis. (There are certain restrictions on f, but this issue does not arise in the "well-behaved" functions in this unit.)

You might add an additional piece to the general principle:

> **If you start with a function, its accumulation function is an antiderivative of the original function.**

More than One Antiderivative

Before leaving this context, ask, Is there any other function that is an antiderivative of the speed function $s(t) = 8.8t$? Students should recall that there are infinitely many choices, such as $g(t) = 4.4t^2 + 100$. You might introduce the "+ C" notation often used to represent this principle. For instance, students might write the general antiderivative for the speed function as $g(t) = 4.4t^2 + C$. Identifying a particular value for this constant will come into play in the final solution of the solar energy problem.

How can you tell that $d(t) = 4.4t^2$ is the right antiderivative in this case? As needed, help students see that the desired antiderivative has the value 0 at $t = 0$, because at 0 seconds the car has not gone anywhere.

Antiderivatives and Integrals

Tell students that another name for antiderivative is *indefinite integral*. This term is commonly used in calculus. (There are other kinds of integrals, which we won't study formally in this unit, though the unit does lay the groundwork for students to understand the definite integral as well.) Because the term *antiderivative* is unambiguous and so descriptive, it's the term used in this unit.

Summary of Derivative Rules

By now, the class should have compiled quite a list of derivative rules and principles. This might be a good time to call their attention to the class poster and ask them to review what they have learned so far. They should bring out all of these ideas, and any others they may have posted:

- They have formulas for the derivatives of various powers of x (at least through x^4).
- They have established the principle that multiplying a function by a constant multiplies its derivative by that constant.
- They have found that the derivative of the sum of two functions is the sum of the derivatives of those functions. (You might ask, Does this principle extend to sums of more than two functions?)
- They have found that the derivative of a constant function or term is zero.
- They have established that if they start with a function and construct a corresponding accumulation function, the new function is an antiderivative of the first function. If they take the derivative of that new function, they get back to the original function.

Ask the class to synthesize these ideas: What kinds of functions can you differentiate by combining these rules and principles? Help students see that they now have the tools for finding the derivatives of polynomial functions (at least through degree 4), which leads in to the next activity.

Key Questions

What does the linear speed graph in this situation imply about the car's acceleration?
How could you use your data or the geometry of the graph to get an algebraic rule for the distance traveled as a function of t?
What is the derivative of this function?
What kinds of functions can you differentiate by combining these rules and principles?

Polynomial Derivatives

Intent

Students find derivatives and antiderivatives of polynomial functions.

Mathematics

This activity generalizes derivatives and antiderivatives as decontextualized functions. The goal is for students to develop some facility with the mechanics of finding derivatives and antiderivatives for polynomial functions.

Progression

Students find the derivatives or antiderivatives of several polynomial functions, explain why functions have more than one antiderivative, and then find multiple antiderivatives for a particular function.

Approximate Time

30 to 40 minutes

Classroom Organization

Individuals, followed by whole-class discussion

Doing the Activity

Before students begin, you might take a moment to clarify the notation for derivatives. For example, in the discussion following *Down the Drain,* students worked with a function of the form $f(x) = 2x^2$ and found its derivative, which they likely expressed as $f'(x) = 4x$. Note that this function can also be written as $y = 2x^2$. Tell students that in this case, the derivative can be written simply as $y' = 4x$. They should use whichever notation best fits the given situation.

Discussing and Debriefing the Activity

For Questions 1, 3, and 4, have students check their answers with one another and discuss any difficulties or conflicts that arise. Generate additional examples if it seems warranted.

Question 2 revisits the idea of constant terms, introduced in *Summer Job.* Students should see that a polynomial (like other functions) has more than one antiderivative, because functions that differ by a constant have the same derivative. Thus, any constant term can be added to an antiderivative to get another antiderivative. If it feels useful, remind students of the "+ C" notation for antiderivatives. For instance, they might write their answer to Question 3a as

$$F(x) = \frac{x^4}{4} + C.$$

Area and Distance

Intent

Students examine relationships among distance, speed, and acceleration.

Mathematics

This activity provides yet another look at the falling-object problem, tying together the antiderivative distance function and the area under the speed graph. This activity creates the context students will use in *A Fundamental Relationship* to establish the **fundamental theorem of calculus.**

Progression

Examining a graph of speed as a function of time, students must explain the relationship between speed and acceleration, and verify the equation for distance fallen, using antiderivatives. Students find the area under the speed graph for several intervals and explain why their results are consistent with the formula obtained as an antiderivative. Finally, they graph the distance fallen as a function of time. The subsequent discussion highlights the equivalence between the area under a speed graph and an antiderivative of the speed function.

Approximate Time

30 minutes for activity (at home or in class)
10 minutes for discussion

Classroom Organization

Individuals, followed by whole-class discussion

Doing the Activity

This activity needs no introduction.

Discussing and Debriefing the Activity

For Question 1, students should be able to say that acceleration measures the rate of change of speed. This means the acceleration function is the derivative of the speed function, which they can demonstrate in this case.

The reverse relationship is more difficult. If acceleration is the rate of change of speed (that is, its derivative), then speed should be an antiderivative and measure "accumulated acceleration." Don't spend too much time on this; the main purpose of the activity lies in the remaining questions.

The goal of Question 2 is for students to articulate the relationship between speed and distance. This can be expressed in several ways, all of them important. The distance the object falls, measured from time 0, is the accumulation for the speed function. Therefore, the speed function is the derivative of the distance function. This means the distance function must be an antiderivative of the speed function. The constant term is 0 because at time 0 seconds, the object has fallen 0 feet. Be sure students note that the derivative for the function $d(t) = 16t^2$ is the speed function $s = 32t$.

You might also bring out that the formula $d(t)$ can be thought of as follows: During the time interval of the first t seconds, the speed increases linearly from 0 to 32t, so the average speed is 16t. (The average speed is half the final speed only because the speed is changing at a constant rate.) If an object travels for t seconds at an average speed of 16t feet per second, it goes a total distance of $16t \cdot t = 16t^2$ feet.

For Question 3, students should find the areas directly. In part c, for instance, the area is a triangle with a base of 5 and a height of 160 (based on the function), or

$$5 \cdot \frac{160}{2} = 400.$$

Ask for units for this value. Although students found the value 400 as an area, the number actually represents the distance traveled, 400 feet—the result of multiplying feet/second by seconds.

Antiderivatives and the Area Under the Speed Graph

For Question 2, students represented the distances at given values of t analytically as the antiderivative of the speed function. For Question 3, they represented some of these same distances by measuring areas under the speed graph; they have come to interpret the quantity measured by such an area as the product of a rate and a time. Questions 4 and 5 are intended to reinforce their understanding that these two very different processes describe the same quantity.

Presentations for Question 4 should demonstrate this equivalence by showing that the area under the graph of $s(t)$ from 0 to t is the same as the value of the function $d(t)$ for several specific values of t. For example, for Question 3c, students should see that the answer they found, 400 feet, is the value of $d(5)$, and that both represent the distance traveled at 5 seconds.

For Question 5, students' observations about their graphs might include these:

- The graph represents the equation $d(t) = 16t^2$.

- The graph increases ever more rapidly, indicating that the falling object goes further in each time interval and so is moving faster over time.
- The slope of the graph keeps getting steeper, also indicating that the speed is increasing.

In this activity, students have focused on the distance quantity, representing it as the area under a graph and as an antiderivative. In the next activity, they will use the same context, but focus on the *rate at which the distance is changing*. This will lead directly to a statement of the fundamental theorem of calculus.

A Fundamental Relationship

Intent

This activity leads directly to a statement of the fundamental theorem of calculus.

Mathematics

Students examine the rate of growth of the area under a speed curve. The discussion introduces a version of the **fundamental theorem of calculus.**

Progression

Students numerically analyze the rate of growth $d(t)$ of the area under a speed graph $s(t)$ to show that $d'(t) = s(t)$ and to generalize that relationship. The subsequent discussion establishes that the rate of growth of the area under a graph is the same as the value of the function. The discussion states the fundamental theorem of calculus and explains the general relationship between rate and accumulation.

Approximate Time

40 to 45 minutes

Classroom Organization

Small groups or individuals, followed by whole-class discussion

Doing the Activity

Transition students from the previous activity by explaining that they will now be working with the same situation, but with a different focus. In *Area and Distance,* they concentrated on describing the *amount* of distance, as measured by the area under the speed graph. Now they will examine the *rate* at which distance is changing, again by measuring areas under the speed graph.

Students should have no trouble carrying out the mechanics in Questions 1 and 2. They may have some difficulty describing the relationships in Questions 3 to 7, especially as the context becomes more abstract.

If students seem to be moving well through the activity, you might let them finish before beginning discussion. Another option is to interrupt after most or all of them have completed Question 4, discuss the first four questions to establish the key ideas, and then have students finish the remaining questions.

Discussing and Debriefing the Activity

This series of questions leads students directly to a simplified version of the **fundamental theorem of calculus.** Questions 1 to 4 develop the argument in the context of a linear speed function. Questions 5 to 7 extend the reasoning to functions in general.

The Distance-Speed Relationship in a Specific Context

In Questions 1 and 2, students numerically approximate the instantaneous rate of growth of the area function at two points, using smaller and smaller increments to approach the limit at each point. As students present their work, be sure to bring out these key ideas:

- Because the area under a speed graph measures distance, students calculate speed as distance traveled per unit time over each interval, that is, as a distance-time ratio.
- Successively smaller increments enable them to find successively better approximations of the instantaneous speed, and this seems to approach a limiting value.
- Finding the limit of the distance-time ratio at a given time is the same as finding the derivative of the distance function at that time.
- The derivative of a distance-vs.-time function is the speed function.
- The graph itself is the speed function, so its value at any t should be the same as the derivative of the distance function, as determined by the area under the graph.

In essence, the rate at which the area is growing at any time t is the same as the value of the function at that time. This is the principle that enables students to verify their estimates in Questions 1e and 2e. Questions 3 and 4 attempt to elicit the same idea in other forms of expression.

The Distance-Speed Relationship Independent of Context

As students present Question 5, encourage them to adapt the more specific reasoning from Questions 1 and 2 to this more abstract situation. For part a, they might describe the added area as an "almost rectangle" with height $f(x)$ and width $h,$ and thus area $f(x) \cdot h$. For part b, the rate of growth with respect to x entails dividing this change in area by the change in x, namely h. The resulting approximation, $\dfrac{f(x) \cdot h}{h}$, gets closer to $f(x)$ as h decreases because the added area gets "more rectangular." In other words, $A'(x) = f(x)$, which should be the conclusion in Question 5c.

Question 6 completes the generalization by getting students to notice that the rate at which the area function changes is independent of the value of x where the area measurement begins. This is just another way of expressing that a given function has many antiderivatives, all of which return to the same function when differentiated.

Students' explanations should use the same reasoning as in Question 5 but also explain the significance of the "starting value." One important point to emphasize is that the value of k is irrelevant to the derivative $A'(x)$ but not to the value of $A(x)$. At a given value of x, the area is growing at a specific speed that has nothing to do with where the accumulation began. But the amount of area clearly depends on where the accumulation started.

Try to get the class to agree on a simple statement summarizing the ideas in Question 6. The statement might be something like this:

> **Given a function $f(x)$ and a starting value $x = k$, if $A(x)$ is the function measuring the area under the graph of f from k to some value of x, then $A'(x) = f(x)$.**

Then dramatically announce that this principle has an exalted name, the **fundamental theorem of calculus.** Add this statement to the class list of derivative principles, perhaps with a title like "Fifth Period's Version of the Fundamental Theorem of Calculus" (see "The Standard Version of the Fundamental Theorem" below).

Question 7 asks students to restate the theorem in the language they're using to try to solve the two unit problems. A typical answer might be, "If you start with a rate function, the area under its graph is an accumulation function. The derivative of this accumulation function at any point is the value of the rate function at that point." Have students relate their statements to their conclusions from the discussion of *Zero to Sixty*. You may also want to post some version of these statements.

You might point out that earlier in the unit, the class used a different line of reasoning to develop the principle that the derivative of an accumulation function is a rate function. What they have accomplished now is a more rigorous demonstration of that principle, based on the definition of the derivative as an instantaneous rate of change.

The Standard Version of the Fundamental Theorem

The class statement will be a simplified rendition of the fundamental theorem of calculus, so you should probably identify it as "their version." Also, the diagram in Question 6 is imprecise; because the variable x is being used in two different senses, a correct formulation requires a second variable. However, introducing this second variable makes the diagram and the theorem more confusing. Here is a more standard version of the theorem:

Fundamental Theorem of Calculus
Given a function $y = f(x)$, if we define $A(t)$ as the area under the graph of $f(x)$ from some fixed left-hand boundary line $x = a$ to some variable right-hand boundary line $x = t$, then $A'(t) = f(t)$.

Even this statement ignores the details of such issues as continuity or the formalism of defining area. But the statement is correct for most common functions, including polynomial and trigonometric functions.

Supplemental Activity

Parabolic Area **(reinforcement)** has students work through the fundamental theorem of calculus in the context of a specific example.

The Leading Edge

Intent

Students explore growth rates of areas and volumes for some simple geometric figures, preparing them to move directly to a solution of the pyramid unit problem.

Mathematics

The main idea in this activity is that the instantaneous growth rate of the volume of some simple geometric solids is the area of the moving surface perpendicular to the direction of growth. Analogously, the instantaneous growth rate of the area of some simple plane figures is the length of the moving side perpendicular to the direction of growth.

Progression

Students consider the rate at which the area and volume of some simple geometric figures increase as one side of the figure moves. The discussion connects this work with the fundamental theorem of calculus.

Approximate Time

25 to 30 minutes for activity (at home or in class)
10 minutes for discussion

Classroom Organization

Individuals, followed by whole-class discussion

Doing the Activity

This activity requires no introduction.

Discussing and Debriefing the Activity

As students present their results for Questions 1 to 3, have them begin by describing the shape created by the moving boundary. This exercise in visualization can be difficult for some people, both speakers and listeners. In Question 3b, for instance, some students may not recognize that the "empty space" is in fact a cylinder whose length and volume are growing.

Make sure students attach appropriate units to the various lengths, surfaces, and volumes. Whereas most situations in *How Much? How Fast?*—including the two unit

IMP Year 4, *How Much? How Fast?* Unit, Teacher's Guide

© 2012 Interactive Mathematics Program

74

problems—deal with rates with respect to time, here the rates are expressed with respect to distance. For example, the growth rate of the shed in Question 2 is in cubic feet per foot.

Several questions relate the *rate* of growth to the *amount* of growth. This is a key idea and warrants some discussion. It revisits the idea of rate × unit = amount, which has been developed in this unit using a variable other than time as the unit of comparison. It also reflects the relationship between rate and accumulation that has been a recent focus.

Two important features should come out in the discussion of Question 4. First, the moving boundary (edge or surface) is straight or flat. Second, it moves in a direction perpendicular to itself.

One useful application of this general growth principle is that it yields formulas for the areas or volumes of several common geometric figures. If the cross-sectional area perpendicular to the direction of growth is constant, as in a right prism or cylinder, the formula emerges algebraically. If the area is variable, as in a pyramid or cone, the formula can be found using simple calculus. Conclude the discussion by having students state formulas for the area of a rectangle, the volume of a box (right rectangular prism), and the volume of a cylinder, and how these formulas emerge from the rate/accumulation relationship.

Back to the Fundamental Theorem

Explore with the class the idea that the units in this activity exhibit a curious feature. In Question 2, for example, if the shed expands upward, its volume grows at a rate of 40 cubic feet per foot. If the roof were raised 3 feet, say, the resulting change in volume would be 120 cubic feet.

Now ask, Could the units of the rate be expressed another way? Students might respond that 40 cubic feet ÷ 1 foot = 40 square feet. But this is precisely the area of the moving surface! Have them repeat the calculation in the other cases to see whether they get the same result.

This discovery provides another insight into the fundamental theorem of calculus. Have students revisit the diagram in Question 5 of *A Fundamental Relationship,* and ask, At what rate is the area under the graph increasing as *x* increases by a small amount *h*? The area increment is roughly $f(x) \cdot h$, and the rate of change entails dividing this by h, leaving (approximately) $f(x)$—which is the length of the boundary line! In other words, if we envision the boundary line moving to the right, it sweeps out new area at a rate equal to its length. This observation provides another, more visual way to think about this powerful theorem. (*Note:* This same principle reappears in more advanced calculus applications, such as finding the volume of a torus.)

Pyramids and Energy

Intent

In these activities, students complete their solutions to the unit problems.

Mathematics

Students solve the first of the two unit problems by using the concept of antiderivatives to develop volume formulas for several solids. They then plan how to apply the concepts they've learned to the solar energy problem. First they learn how to use radian measure and how it applies to trigonometric functions. They then use approximations of derivative graphs for several trigonometric functions to develop formulas for the derivatives, leading to a solution of the solar energy problem.

Progression

In *Filling the Reservoir,* students find an exact solution to the initial unit problem, *Building the Pyramid.* In *A Pyramid of Bright Ideas*, they plan how to similarly use the concept of an antiderivative to explore and solve the solar energy problem.

In preparation for working with the derivatives of trigonometric functions, *Trying a New Angle* and *Different Angles* introduce radian measure and extend that concept to trigonometric functions.

A Solar Formula reveals that solving the solar energy problem will require finding an antiderivative for the function $P = 2400 \sin\left(\frac{\pi}{12}t\right)$. The class begins by using approximation in *A Sine Derivative* to get a graph for the derivative of the sine function, observing that this graph looks roughly like the cosine graph. They prove this conjecture in *A Derivative Proof*, basing their reasoning upon the geometry in the definition of the sine.

Because the derivative of the sine function is the cosine function, students might hope that the reverse is also true—that the derivative of the cosine function is the sine function. In *A Cosine Derivative,* they use approximation to get a graph for the derivative of the cosine function. They see that this graph looks roughly like the negative of the sine graph and then see how this relationship can be proved from their result about the sine function.

Knowing that the negative of the cosine function is the antiderivative of the sine function, students proceed to adjust the cosine function further to deal with the coefficients in the desired derivative, $P = 2400 \sin\left(\frac{\pi}{12}t\right)$. The first concern is with the "inside coefficient," $\frac{\pi}{12}$. In *The Inside Story,* students examine the derivative of the function $y = \cos(2x)$ to get a sense of how an inside coefficient affects the derivative of a trigonometric function. Then they make a final adjustment to deal with the "outside coefficient," 2400.

Students summarize the steps that were required for the development of the solution for the solar energy problem in *A Solar Summary*. They then further describe what they have learned in the unit in *"How Much? How Fast?" Portfolio*.

Filling the Reservoir
A Pyramid of Bright Ideas
Trying a New Angle
Different Angles
A Solar Formula
A Sine Derivative
A Derivative Proof
A Cosine Derivative
The Inside Story
A Solar Summary
"How Much? How Fast?" Portfolio

Filling the Reservoir

Intent

Students use antiderivatives to find formulas for the volumes of pyramids and cones.

Mathematics

This activity brings students back to the first unit problem, introduced in *Building the Pyramid*, involving the volume of a pyramid. Rather than dealing directly with volume, students focus on how the volume changes, using the scenario of filling a pyramid-shaped reservoir with water. In other words, the problem is now framed in a way that allows students to apply their new ideas about rate and accumulation. The discussion extends this problem to developing formulas for the volumes of pyramids and cones.

Progression

Students examine the *Building the Pyramid* volume problem from a dynamic perspective, looking at how the volume changes as the pyramid is filled with water. Students will conclude that the rate at which the volume changes with respect to time t is equal to t^2. The discussion leads them to find the total volume using the antiderivative and, ultimately, to use this approach to find general volume formulas for pyramids and cones.

Approximate Time

25 minutes for activity (at home or in class)
15 minutes for discussion

Classroom Organization

Individuals, followed by whole-class discussion

Doing the Activity

For Question 1a, you might remind students that 5 minutes is $\frac{1}{12}$ of an hour, so the reservoir's depth will increase by $\frac{1}{12}$ of a foot. Although this is equal to 1 inch, students are better off thinking in terms of feet and expressing the volume in cubic feet.

Additionally, you might suggest that students picture the layer of "new water" added during these 5 minutes. They should see that this layer of water is, more or less, in the shape of a rectangular solid, with a square base 30 feet on each side and a depth of $\frac{1}{12}$ of a foot. So the amount of water added is roughly

$$30 \cdot 30 \cdot \frac{1}{12} = 75 \text{ cubic feet.}$$

Discussing and Debriefing the Activity

You may want to have students go through Question 1 and one or two examples from Question 2 in detail. It may help to put the estimated rates into a table as a function of the time at which they are computed. This table could form the basis for conjecturing a rule for the rate of filling.

Another way to develop the rule for Question 3 is to visualize the new "layer" of water added over a small interval. Each such layer is approximately a rectangular solid, with a square base and a small height, whose volume is roughly the product of the area of the base with the height. This relates directly to the modeling of the pyramid's volume with cubes in *Building the Pyramid*.

The ideas from *The Leading Edge* suggest a third approach. The volume of this pyramid of water is being generated by a flat base (the surface of the water) that is growing perpendicularly to its plane. Consequently, the rate of growth of the volume should be exactly the area of the boundary surface. This is a square whose area at any time t is simple to describe.

These analyses should lead students to recognize that at a time t hours after the reservoir begins to fill, the rate at which water is being added is approximately t^2 cubic feet per hour. (In fact, the rate is exactly t^2, but a formal demonstration of this requires limits and is not needed here.)

From Rate to Volume

Ask, **What does this rate say about the volume function $V(t)$ that represents the amount of water after t hours?** If necessary, remind students of their extensive work with rate and accumulation functions. They should see that they have shown that $V'(t) = t^2$.

What does this say about $V(t)$ itself? Students should be able to explain that because $y = t^2$ is the derivative of $V(t)$, then $V(t)$ must be an antiderivative for the function $y = t^2$. They can then easily compute the volume function as $V(t) = \frac{t^3}{3}$.

If it doesn't come up, point out that there are other functions with the desired derivative, such as $V(t) = \dfrac{t^3}{3} + 10$. Simply use the fact that $V(0) = 0$ to establish that $V(t) = \dfrac{t^3}{3}$ is the particular antiderivative wanted here.

The Volume of the Original Pyramid

Now ask, **What does this formula for $V(t)$ say about the volume of water in the reservoir when it is full?** Students should see that this volume must be $V(100)$, which is $\dfrac{100^3}{3}$, or approximately 333,333 (cubic feet).

Connect this result back to the original pyramid-volume problem, and compare the exact value with the approximated value found in *Building the Pyramid*. The opening unit problem has now been solved exactly, and the original estimates turn out to have been quite accurate.

In the end, the exact volume was found as an antiderivative of the function describing the rate at which the volume was changing.

Pyramids and Cones

Caution students that the volume formula they found, $V(t) = \dfrac{t^3}{3}$, is based on a pyramid whose base length is the same as its height (or depth). They might wonder whether the formula would work for all pyramids. Tell them that the ideas from *The Leading Edge* provide a way to explore this question and to search for a volume formula for cones as well.

Formula for the Volume of a Right Pyramid

This explanation will be restricted to right pyramids with square bases. Here is a side view of such a pyramid, oriented base upward. The solid version is the pyramid at one moment; the dotted version shows how it has grown after some time has passed. The vertical lines indicate the heights, and the horizontal lines indicate the bases.

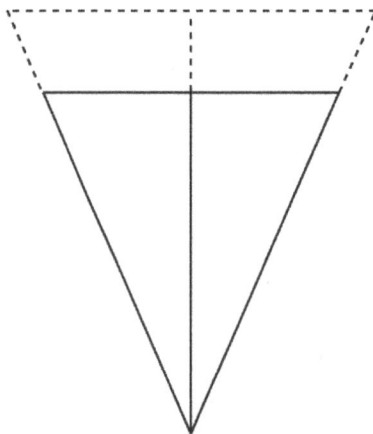

Start by displaying this diagram and checking whether students understand what it represents. A key observation is that the pyramid's growth fits the conditions in *The Leading Edge:* the moving boundary is flat and is growing perpendicularly to its plane. The volume grows with respect to the height.

Ask, **How would you describe the relationship between the base *b* and the height *h*?** Students should recognize that the similar figures mean that the ratio of base to height remains constant as the pyramid grows, even though the values of *b* and *h* both change. Suggest naming this constant ratio, say $k = \dfrac{h}{b}$.

Students can now use simple algebra to create an expression for the area of the growing surface, which they know to be the derivative of the volume function, in terms of the height. The result should be $V' = \dfrac{1}{k^2}h^2$. Finding the appropriate antiderivative and substituting for *k* yields the formula $V = \dfrac{1}{3}b^2h$. It might be worthwhile comparing this result to the more restrictive formula found in *Filling the Reservoir*.

You might also suggest comparing this formula to that for the volume of a right square prism (a box with two square ends).

Formula for the Volume of a Cone

At this point, you could simply turn students loose to find a formula for the volume of a cone. The side view diagram is identical to that for a pyramid, and the only difference in the calculations involves substituting the area of a circle for that of a square. The final result of $V = \dfrac{1}{3}\pi r^2 h$ can be compared to the volume of a cylinder with essentially the same result.

Key Questions

What does this rate say about the volume function $V(t)$ that represents the amount of water after t hours? What does this say about $V(t)$ itself? What does this formula for $V(t)$ say about the volume of water in the reservoir when it is full?

A Pyramid of Bright Ideas

Intent

Students reflect upon how they can apply the ideas they have learned so far to the central unit problems.

Mathematics

In the first part of this writing assignment, students summarize their work on the pyramid-volume problem and reflect on what they have learned about rates and accumulation. In the second part, they review what they know about the solar-collector problem and try to describe a solution path.

Progression

Students summarize the key ideas that led to the solution of the pyramid problem and write out a strategy for solving the problem from *Warming Up*. The subsequent discussion helps to identify the remaining subproblems for that unit problem.

Approximate Time

25 minutes for activity (at home or in class)
10 minutes for discussion

Classroom Organization

Individuals, followed by small-group and whole-class discussion

Doing the Activity

This activity requires no introduction.

Discussing and Debriefing the Activity

Use the discussion of Question 1 as an opportunity to emphasize key ideas about rate and accumulation. Focus on the fact that as the reservoir fills, there is a simple formula for the rate of growth of its volume, that is, for the derivative of the volume function. This means the volume itself can be found using an antiderivative of that derivative.

Tell students that a reexamination of the solar energy problem is the focus of the balance of the unit. In Question 2, they should have reviewed the two graphs they already have for this situation. This graph (created for *Warming Up*) shows the power of the solar energy system, or the rate at which energy is being absorbed. You may wish to remind students that watts are a measure of the rate of energy transfer.

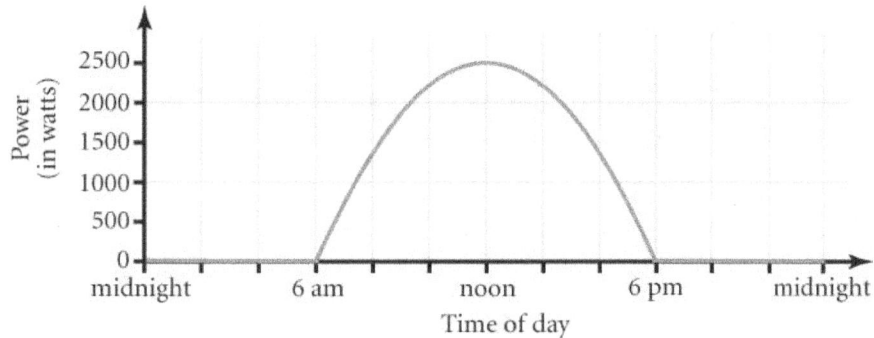

Students also have a partial graph of accumulated energy, created as part of the discussion of *Total Heat.*

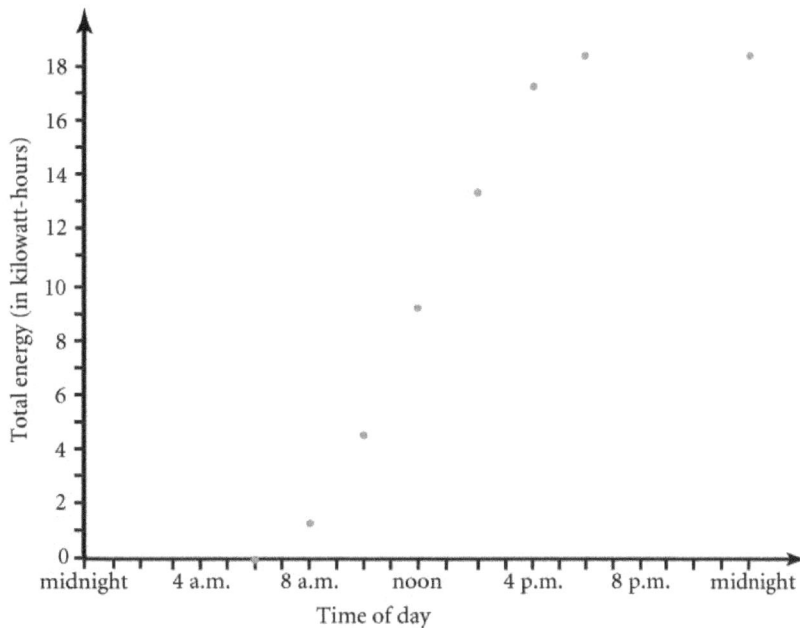

Point out that the accumulation graph is always rising, and connect this with the fact that the rate graph is always positive. Students might also note that the accumulation graph is steepest at noon, which is the time at which the rate graph is at a maximum.

More generally, help students to articulate the principle that the rate graph is the derivative of the accumulation graph.

Prompt them to share their thinking by asking, What strategies might we use to solve the *Warming Up* problem? Have students share their strategies in small groups. Ask each group to compile their ideas and come up with a single plan for solving the problem.

Ask a couple of groups to explain their plans to the class. As they present, you might list the tools that still need to be developed in order to carry out the plans.

There are two key steps in the solution:

Step 1. Find a precise equation for the graph of the rate of energy gain.
Step 2. Find an antiderivative for this function.

Key Question

What strategies might we use to solve the *Warming Up* problem?

Supplemental Activity

***Ana on the Train* (reinforcement)** applies the fundamental theorem of calculus to another motion problem, this time with variable acceleration.

Trying a New Angle

Intent

Students develop the radian measure.

Mathematics

This activity guides students through development of the concept of **radian** measure and relates radian and degree measures. This idea will be important for writing an exact equation to describe the power graph from *Warming Up*. The answer is, "Yes, but . . ." Neither the height (amplitude) nor the length (related to period) of this graph match those of the function $y = \sin t$. Writing an equation that works may seem simple using degrees for angle measurement. While this is convenient in some practical applications, it is awkward in many mathematical contexts, and in calculus in particular.

To see why, consider this graph of a portion of $y = \sin t$, with t measured in degrees:

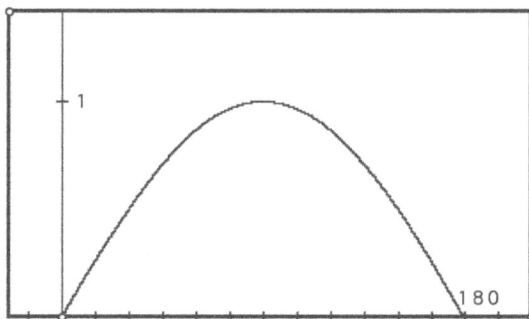

When a slope triangle is constructed at some point on this graph, the "rise over run" ratio compares a pure number to degrees, and the resulting slope is in rather strange units. Considering the area under a portion of the curve is even more problematic, resulting in the product of a pure number and degrees.

What is needed is a form of the sine function that is independent of degrees or any other arbitrary measurement unit. Fortunately, there is another simple way of measuring angles that solves this dilemma. If t is measured in radians, the graph of this same portion of $y = \sin t$ looks like this:

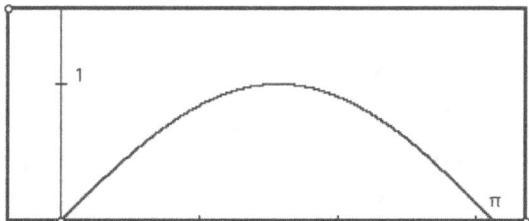

The horizontal and vertical scales are identical, and they're pure number scales. Consequently, any measures of slope (derivative) or area (antiderivative) are directly meaningful. Another way to say this is that the argument (the angle) and the value of the sine function are in the same units, just as we would expect when graphing $y = 2x + 3$, for example. By extension, using radians enables all the trigonometric functions to be defined in the abstract as functions of pure numbers without reference to angles, which makes trigonometric functions more powerful as mathematical tools.

In *A Derivative Proof,* students will find the derivative of the sine function. The proof depends on being able to measure both an angle and its subtended arc length in the same units. This ability is another consequence of using radian measure, as students will discover in *Trying a New Angle*.

Progression

After sketching sectors for circles with central angles measuring 1 radian—first estimating the measurements and then calculating them—students write a definition for *radian.* They also develop and then practice processes for converting between radian and degree measures.

Approximate Time

40 minutes

Classroom Organization

Groups or individuals, followed by whole-class discussion

Doing the Activity

You might introduce this activity by simply explaining that its purpose is to develop an essential tool for solving the solar energy unit problem. Its usefulness will gradually become apparent over the next few days, beginning with *Different Angles*. If students work in groups, have each student do his or her own work.

When students are ready to do the "Application" problems, interrupt them to explain how to toggle their calculators between degree and radian mode, and emphasize the need to remember this when doing calculations.

Discussing and Debriefing the Activity

Students should have constructed reasonable definitions for **radian,** something like "the measure of a central angle in a circle that marks an arc the same length as the radius." They should also have noted that this works for a circle of any size. Bring out that although the definition of *radian* is framed in terms of central angles, any angle can be thought of as a central angle simply by creating a unit circle with the angle's vertex as its center.

Spend a little time on the question, **What is the equivalence between radians and degrees?** Help students become familiar with a few basic equivalents by asking such questions as, **What is the radian measure for a 90° (central) angle? A 45° angle? A 270° angle?** Focus on the idea that each of these angles is a simple fraction of a full turn, so that the intercepted arcs are fractions of the full circumference. Explain that we usually express these answers in terms of π, rather than decimal approximations, to reinforce this relationship.

In the reverse direction, reinforce students' discovery of how big 1 radian is (a bit less than one-sixth of a full circle, or a little less than 60°). You might ask for the degree equivalents of some simple examples. **What is the degree measure for π radians? For $\dfrac{\pi}{3}$ radians?**

Question 10 provides a good opportunity to explore these relationships further. You might ask, **How could we express radian and degree measures as a proportion?** The solution to Question 10 can be expressed as either a conversion formula or a proportion, and it ties in the calculation of arc length as well.

Another provocative question is, **We write 30° using the unit symbol for degrees. Why don't we use some sort of unit symbol for its radian equivalent, $\dfrac{\pi}{6}$?** The beauty of using radians for measuring angles is that, because they are the ratio of a length (an arc) to another length (a radius), they are unitless measures—that is, pure numbers. This is what makes radians so useful for graphing trigonometric functions, an idea students will explore in *Different Angles*. For now, just bring out this unusual property of radians as pure numbers that measure the size of angles.

Key Questions

What is the equivalence between radians and degrees?
What is the radian measure for a 90° (central) angle? A 45° angle? A 270° angle?

What is the degree measure for π radians? For $\dfrac{\pi}{3}$ radians?

How could we express radian and degree measure as a proportion?
We write 30° using the unit symbol for degrees. Why don't we use some

sort of unit symbol for its radian equivalent, $\dfrac{\pi}{6}$?

Different Angles

Intent

Students extend the radian measure to trigonometric functions.

Mathematics

Students practice using radian measure and applying it to the sine function to prepare for finding an exact formula for the solar power graph.

Progression

Students convert several angle measures between degrees and radians and then evaluate trigonometric functions for angles measured in radians. They also sketch a graph of the sine function using radian measure and make some observations about derivatives of this function.

Approximate Time

30 to 40 minutes for activity (at home or in class)
15 minutes for discussion

Classroom Organization

Individuals, followed by whole-class discussion

Doing the Activity

This activity needs no introduction.

Discussing and Debriefing the Activity

For Question 2, students may reason, for example, that an angle of 60° is one-sixth of a full turn, so it represents 2π/6 radians, which simplifies to $\frac{\pi}{3}$ radians. Similarly, 30° is one-twelfth of a circle and 300° is five-sixths of a circle. Students might use the fact that 30° is half of 60° and that 300° is five times 60°.

One approach to Question 3 is to use the fact that π radians is equal to 180° and then apply each fraction to 180°. For instance, $\frac{3\pi}{4}$ radians is $\frac{3}{4}$ of 180°, which is

135°. Other approaches include using the equations that students developed in *Trying a New Angle* or setting up and solving proportions.

As students present the graph for Question 6, acknowledge that the horizontal scale is a bit tricky; because the key values take place at $\frac{\pi}{6}$, $\frac{\pi}{2}$, and so on, students need to estimate these places along the horizontal axis. The graph will be roughly three times as wide as it is high, because the value of sin x goes from −1 to 1.

For Question 7, if the graph is drawn accurately, the tangent line at the origin should make an angle of 45° with the axes, and thus its slope is 1. You might inform students that in fact, the slope is exactly 1, as they will soon see.

Ask, **What does this slope represent in terms of the function $y = \sin x$?** Bring out, as needed, that this is the derivative of the function at the point where x = 0.

Are there are any other values of the derivative that are easy to find?

Students might note that the graph flattens out at $x = \frac{\pi}{2}$, so the derivative there is 0, and by symmetry, the derivative at $x = \pi$ is −1.

Finally, for Question 8, students should see that if they used degrees and used the same numeric scale for both axes, the graph would be *very* wide (360 units!), yet still only 2 units high. Also, the angle and slope of the tangent line at the origin would be much smaller, because the vertical gain would be spread out over a much greater horizontal amount.

You might point out that using radians has thus provided an advantage similar to the use of *e* as a base for exponents—it has made a derivative come out very nicely. Other advantages will become evident over the next few activities.

Key Question

What does this slope represent in terms of the function $y = \sin x$?

A Solar Formula

Intent

Students look for an equation for the power graph from *Warming Up.*

Mathematics

In the discussion that followed *A Pyramid of Bright Ideas*, the class recognized that in order to solve the central unit problem, they would need to find a precise equation for the graph of the rate of the energy gain and then find an antiderivative for that function. Now they complete the first of those two steps, finding the equation. To facilitate finding an antiderivative later, they use radian measure.

Progression

Students find an equation, using radian measure, for the rate at which the solar-collection system from *Warming Up* absorbs energy. In the subsequent discussion, they speculate about how to find an antiderivative for this function.

Approximate Time

35 minutes

Classroom Organization

Small groups or individuals, followed by whole-class discussion

Doing the Activity

This activity completes the first part of the two-step plan developed (during the discussion following *A Pyramid of Bright Ideas*) for solving the solar energy problem: finding an equation for the power graph from *Warming Up.* To remind students that the graph involves the sine function, you might review how that graph was developed.

Adjusting the sine function to use radian measure may be challenging, because many students have had minimal experience with radians. The key is to recognize that a complete cycle of $y = \sin x$ occurs as x goes from 0 to 2π (that is, the period is 2π). In the function $P(t)$, when $t = 12$ (that is, at 6 p.m.), the sine function should be halfway through its cycle. You may have to help students see that this means that when $t = 12$, the input to the sine function should be π, so the function should use a coefficient of $\frac{\pi}{12}$ for t.

Students will probably be clear that they need to multiply the sine function by 2400 to get the desired maximum. Help them adjust the input to the sine function, as just described, so they get the equation $P = 2400 \sin\left(\dfrac{\pi}{12}t\right)$ to represent the graph for values between $t = 0$ and $t = 12$. You might have students graph this function on their calculators (using radian mode!) to confirm that it gives the right graph.

[*Note:* Writing $\sin\left(\dfrac{\pi}{12}t\right)$ instead of $\sin\left(\dfrac{\pi t}{12}\right)$ will help students identify $\dfrac{\pi}{12}$ as a coefficient for t.]

Discussing and Debriefing the Activity

A good way to start the discussion is to ask, In your equation, what are the units for t? For P? For the area under the curve? Help students recognize that this equation for the power function does not involve degrees, only hours and watts; consequently, there is no confusion over units. Just as with the slope they calculated for the sine function, the use of radians simplifies the situation.

Help students recall that the area under the curve represents energy (in watt-hours) and that they found a numeric estimate for the total energy accumulation in *Total Heat*.

What's Next?

Students have just completed Step 1 of the two-step solution process described in the discussion following *A Pyramid of Bright Ideas* for getting an equation for the energy-accumulation graph. Review this solution process with them. Step 2 is to find an antiderivative for the function defining P.

How might you go about finding an antiderivative for the function $P = 2400$ $\sin\left(\dfrac{\pi}{12}t\right)$? Let students brainstorm ideas about this. You might point out that they have an approximate graph of the accumulation function, from the discussion of *Total Heat*, shown again here.

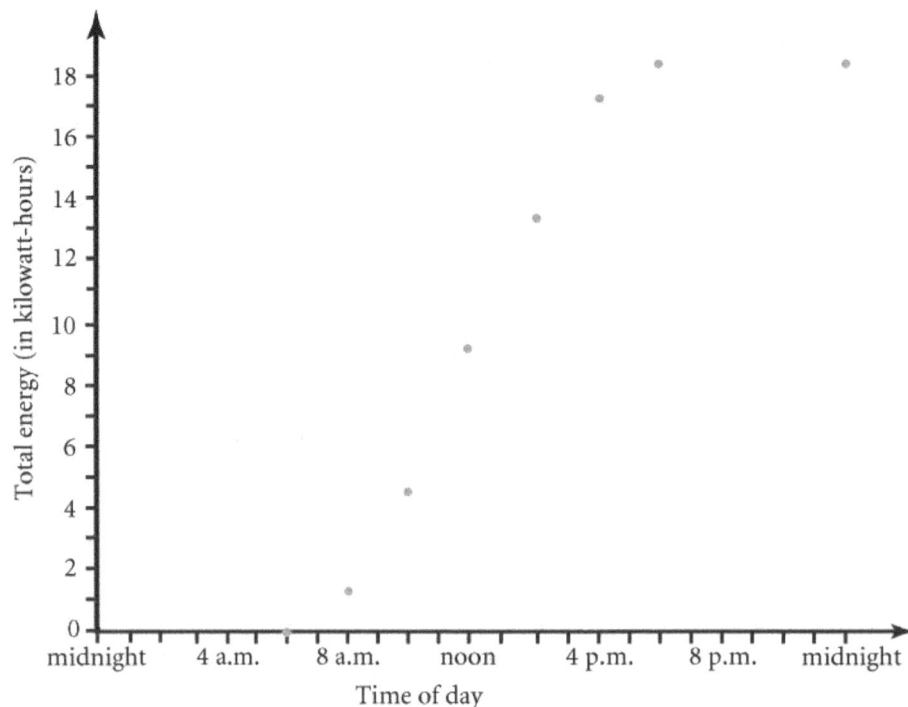

They may notice that the relevant portion of this graph, from 6 a.m. to 6 p.m., looks vaguely like part of the graph of the sine function, which might suggest starting the search for an antiderivative by finding the derivative of the sine function itself.

You might also suggest that they could begin by finding an antiderivative for the "plain" sine function, $y = \sin x$, and then make adjustments for the factors 2400 and $\dfrac{\pi}{12}$.

The balance of the unit is based on the idea of starting by looking at the derivative of the sine function, but if students have other ideas for how to start, you might alter the plan and follow their lead. (In that case, you may want to review the overview of the original plan for this section as described in the teaching notes for *Pyramids and Energy*.) If you want to encourage students to start with the sine function as a first guess for its own antiderivative, you might point out that the function $y = e^x$ is its own antiderivative, so the sine function might also have this property.

Key Questions

In your equation, what are the units for *t*? For *P*? For the area under the curve?

How might you go about finding an antiderivative for the function $P = 2400 \sin\left(\dfrac{\pi}{12}t\right)$?

A Sine Derivative

Intent

Students begin to search for the derivative of the sine function.

Mathematics

Students use approximation to get a graph of the derivative of the sine function. The shape of this graph leads them to a conjecture that the cosine is the derivative of the sine function.

Progression

Given a graph of the sine function using radian measure, students estimate the derivative for nine different angles. They plot those results and consider what the new graph suggests for the derivative of the sine function. The subsequent discussion establishes that the derivative of the sine function resembles the cosine function.

Approximate Time

25 to 35 minutes for activity (at home or in class)
10 minutes for discussion

Classroom Organization

Individuals, followed by whole-class discussion

Doing the Activity

This activity requires no introduction.

Discussing and Debriefing the Activity

You might have volunteers give their answers for the various cases in Question 1 and plot all the results on a single set of axes with equal scales. Note that the use of radian measure makes this easier to do and also yields meaningful area units (since each grid square is 1 by 1). If there are significant disagreements about the results, discuss the issues involved and ask for any special techniques students used (such as symmetry).

It's crucial that students see that although $\frac{\pi}{4}$ is halfway between 0 and $\frac{\pi}{2}$, the derivative at $x = \frac{\pi}{4}$ is not halfway between the derivatives at $x = 0$ and $x = \frac{\pi}{2}$. That fact suggests that the resulting graph has the curved shape of the cosine function rather than consisting of a sequence of up-and-down line segments.

You might specifically note that at $x = 0$, the graph appears to have a tangent line at an angle of 45°, so the slope appears to be 1.

If students have constructed the graph reasonably carefully, they should conclude in Question 3 that the derivative of the sine function is probably the cosine function.

A Derivative Proof

Intent

Students prove that the derivative of the sine function is the cosine function.

Mathematics

Using the geometry inherent in the definition of the sine function, students prove the conjecture that arose from viewing an approximate graph of the derivative of the sine function in *A Sine Derivative*.

Progression

Students examine the development of a proof that the derivative of the sine function is the cosine function. The subsequent discussion highlights the role of radian measure in the proof.

Approximate Time

5 minutes for introduction
25 minutes for activity (at home or in class)
10 minutes for discussion

Classroom Organization

Individuals, followed by whole-class discussion

Doing the Activity

The goal of this activity is to prove the conjecture that the derivative of the sine function is the cosine function. You might introduce the activity by commenting that because trigonometric functions are defined geometrically, it makes sense that finding their derivatives should also involve geometry.

Then ask, **How would you find the derivative of sin x at a particular point (x, sin x)?** Use a diagram like this one to illustrate the key ideas:

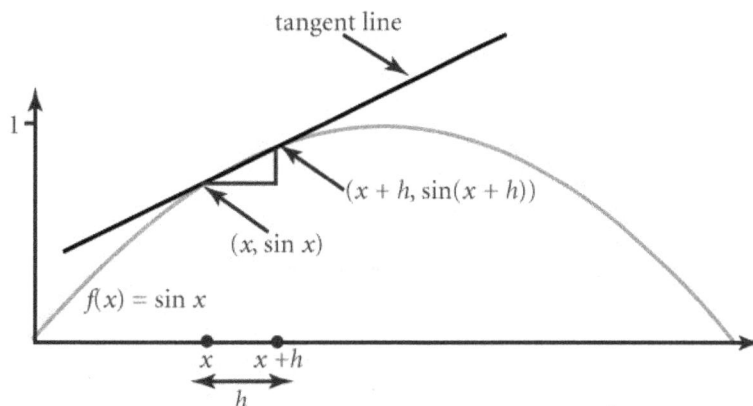

Basically, students should recognize that they want to estimate the slope of the tangent line, which involves finding a "rise over run" ratio. In the diagram, the rise is $\sin(x + h) - \sin x$ and the run is simply h [or $(x + h) - x$]. Thus, students' goal is to examine the ratio $\dfrac{\sin(x + h) - \sin x}{h}$.

Discussing and Debriefing the Activity

You might have volunteers explain each step in the process, based on the relevant parts of the diagram, which is reproduced here:

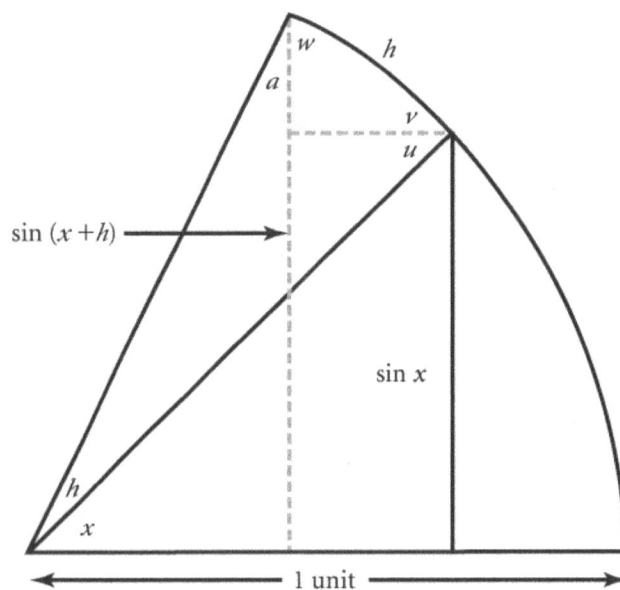

For Question 1, the relevant portion is shown here:

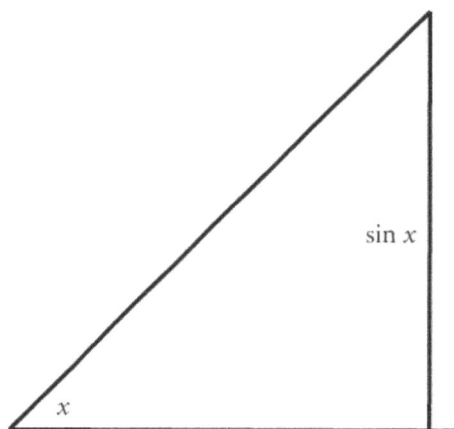

We have $\sin x = \dfrac{\text{opposite}}{\text{hypotenuse}}$ (as with any angle), but the hypotenuse of this triangle is a radius of the circle, so its length is 1. Therefore, the "opposite" is simply $\sin x$, as labeled.

Similar reasoning applies in Question 2, using the next diagram, in which the angle in the lower left of the large right triangle is the sum $x + h$. Again, the hypotenuse is a radius, so $\sin (x + h)$ is simply the "opposite," as labeled.

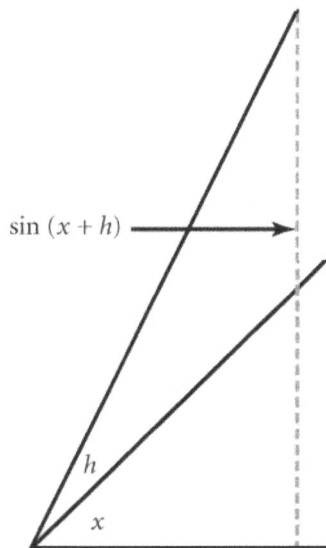

You might use Question 3 as an opportunity to point out the crucial role of radian measure. If students were not using radian measure, the length of the small arc would be $\dfrac{h}{360} \cdot 2\pi$ instead of just h, and the formula for the derivative would be much messier.

In Question 4, students need only see that while the entire vertical dashed segment has length $\sin (x + h)$, part of this segment is equal to the solid vertical segment with length $\sin x$. Thus the segment shown as a in the small "triangle" is the difference $\sin (x + h) - \sin x$, so $\dfrac{\sin (x + h) - \sin x}{h}$ is just $\dfrac{a}{h}$, which is equal to $\cos w$ (or $\sin v$), which answers Question 5. For the later discussion, it's important that students see that $\dfrac{\sin (x + h) - \sin x}{h}$ is equal to $\cos w$.

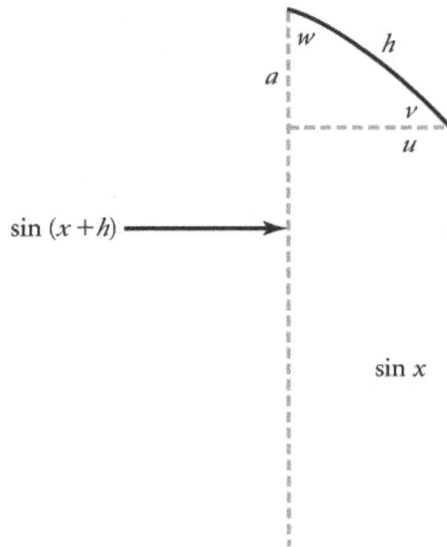

Question 6 may be the most challenging. The hardest part is seeing that the angles *u* and *v* are complementary, because the arc *h* is perpendicular to the radius to the vertex of those angles. Also, angles *x* and *u* are equal, because of parallel line properties, and angles *v* and *w* are complementary because they are the acute angles of a right triangle.

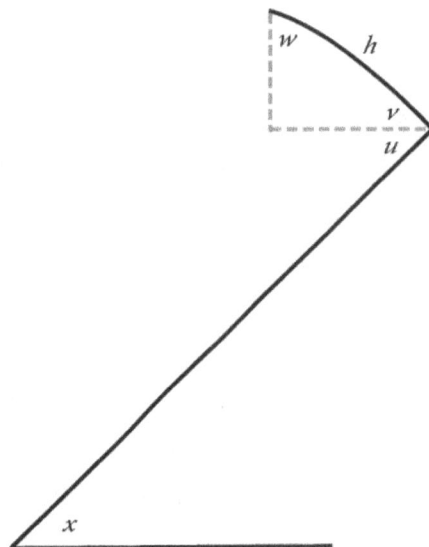

Putting this all together implies that *w = x*. Because students saw in Question 5 that $\dfrac{\sin(x+h) - \sin x}{h}$ = cos *w*, they now have this ratio equal to cos *x*, for Question 7. (The ratio is also the sine of the complement of *x*, but that fact is less useful.)

IMP Year 4, *How Much? How Fast?* Unit, Teacher's Guide

© 2012 Interactive Mathematics Program

99

In summary (Question 8): Except for the assumption that the arc h is a line segment, perpendicular to the radius, this sequence of steps shows that $\frac{\sin(x + h) - \sin x}{h}$ = cos x. As h gets smaller, the assumption becomes more valid.

Thus, the derivative ratio gets closer and closer to cos x, proving that the derivative of the sine function is the cosine function. (*Note:* This proof is valid only if x is an acute angle, but the corresponding fact for other angles follows using the symmetries of the sine and cosine functions.)

You might add this conclusion to the class list of derivative rules:

The derivative of the sine function is the cosine function. That is, if $f(x)$ = sin x, then $f'(x)$ = cos x.

What Next?

Remind students that their goal is to find an antiderivative for the function

$P = 2400 \sin\left(\frac{\pi}{12}t\right)$ from *A Solar Formula*. Instead, they have found an

antiderivative for the cosine function. So there are two pieces left to the puzzle:
- Adjust the result to find a function whose derivative is sine instead of cosine.
- Adjust that result to account for the "outside coefficient" 2400 and the

  "inside coefficient" $\frac{\pi}{12}$. (*Note: The Inside Story* is concerned with treating

  the issue of the inside coefficient.)

Students will begin on the first of these pieces in *A Cosine Derivative*. You might motivate that activity by asking, If the antiderivative of the cosine function is the sine function, what's the antiderivative of the sine function? It's natural to guess that the answer is the cosine function. So students' next task is to find the derivative of the cosine function, perhaps hoping to get sin x as the result. They will see otherwise, but the guess isn't far off.

Students will begin work on the second remaining piece of the puzzle in *The Inside Story*.

Key Questions

How would you find the derivative of sin x at a particular point $(x, \sin x)$? If the antiderivative of the cosine function is the sine function, what's the antiderivative of the sine function?

A Cosine Derivative

Intent

In this activity, which is similar to *A Sine Derivative*, students discover the derivative of the cosine function.

Mathematics

By constructing a sketch of the graph of the cosine function, students observe that it resembles the negative of the sine function. In the follow-up discussion, they see how the conjecture from this activity follows from the corresponding fact for the sine function, using ideas of symmetry and translation.

Progression

Using a graph of the function, students estimate the derivative of cos x for several values of x. They then plot their results and consider what their graph suggests for the derivative of the cosine function. In the subsequent discussion, the class proves that the derivative of the cosine function is the negative of the sine function.

Approximate Time

25 minutes for activity (at home or in class)
10 minutes for discussion

Classroom Organization

Individuals, followed by whole-class discussion

Doing the Activity

This activity requires no introduction.

Discussing and Debriefing the Activity

You may not need to go over this activity in detail. Students may have seen clearly that if $f(x) = \cos x$, then $f'(x)$ seems to be $-\sin x$.

A valuable way to visualize this result is to note that the cosine graph can be obtained by shifting the sine graph 90° (or $\frac{\pi}{2}$ radians) to the left. Therefore, the derivative of the cosine graph can be obtained from the derivative of the sine function by shifting that graph 90° to the left. The derivative of sine is cosine, and if that graph is shifted 90° to the left, the result is the negative of the sine graph.

In the diagram here, points A and B are in similar positions relative to the cosine and sine functions, so their tangent lines are parallel and their derivatives are equal. Point B is on the sine graph, so its derivative is the cosine of its x-value, which is the y-coordinate of point C. This is the same as the y-coordinate of point D, which is the negative of the sine of the x-coordinate at point A.

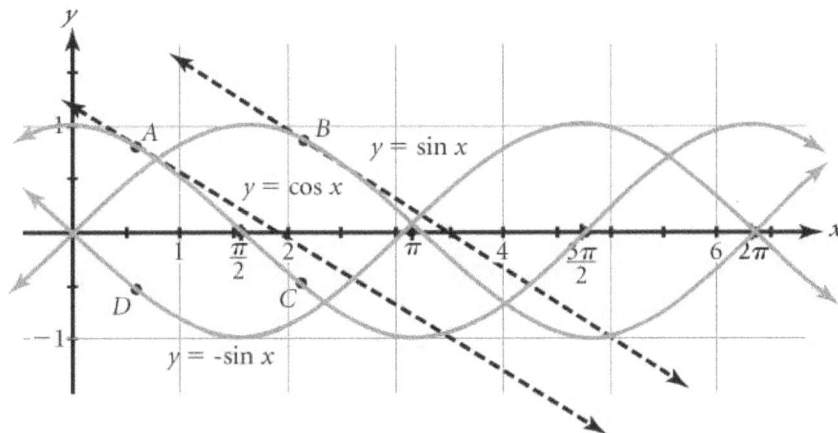

You can now post this conclusion:

The derivative of the cosine function is the negative of the sine function. That is, if $f(x) = \cos x$, then $f'(x) = -\sin x$.

Turning the cosine graph upside down (that is, taking its negative) will change the sign of the derivative at each point on the graph. Here, then, is another useful rule you might post:

The derivative of the negative of the cosine function is the sine function. That is, if $f(x) = -\cos x$, then $f'(x) = \sin x$.

Students have found an antiderivative for the sine function. Unfortunately, their task is not to find an antiderivative for the "plain" sine function, but to find an antiderivative for the function $P = 2400 \sin\left(\dfrac{\pi}{12}t\right)$ from *A Solar Formula.* They now need to do the second of the two tasks posed at the end of the discussion of *A Derivative Proof:* adjust the result to account for the "outside coefficient" 2400 and the "inside coefficient" $\dfrac{\pi}{12}$.

The Inside Story

Intent

Students determine the derivative of the function $y = \cos(2x)$.

Mathematics

Students now use a graphical estimate to determine the derivative of a function of the type $y = \cos(kx)$.

Progression

As in previous activities, students use a graph of a function to estimate and plot the derivative of the function at a number of points and then use their graph to form a conjecture about the derivative of the function. The subsequent discussion explains the result using adjusted "rise over run" diagrams and applies the principle to the equation $f(x) = \cos\left(\dfrac{\pi}{12}x\right)$. Students then complete the solar energy problem by finding the appropriate antiderivative for the function $P = 2400 \sin\left(\dfrac{\pi}{12}t\right)$ and using the antiderivative to find the total energy accumulated. The class compares this result with that from *Total Heat*.

Approximate Time

40 to 45 minutes

Classroom Organization

Groups or individuals, followed by whole-class discussion

Doing the Activity

Students have seen that if $f(x) = -\cos x$, then $f'(x) = \sin x$. Before they tackle the formula for P in all its complexity, ask students, **What function might have as its derivative sin (2x)?** They are likely to guess that $-\cos(2x)$ might work.

You might introduce the activity by asking, **How is the graph of $y = \cos(2x)$ related to the graph of $y = \cos x$?** For instance, if $x = \dfrac{\pi}{3}$, then $\cos x$ is .5, so the point $\left(\dfrac{\pi}{3}, .5\right)$ is on the graph of $y = \cos x$. The corresponding point on the graph of

$y = \cos(2x)$ is $\left(\frac{\pi}{6}, .5\right)$, because $\cos\left(2 \cdot \frac{\pi}{6}\right)$ is the same as $\cos\left(\frac{\pi}{3}\right)$. Thus, the graph in the activity is a "horizontal compression" of the graph of $y = \cos x$.

Discussing and Debriefing the Activity

Students should see that the resulting graph of derivatives is like the negative of the sine function, but different in two ways:

- The derivative graph is "compressed horizontally." It goes through a complete cycle in the interval from $x = 0$ to $x = \pi$.
- The graph is "stretched vertically." Its highest value is at $y = 2$, and its lowest is at $y = -2$.

The first item may not be at all surprising, but students are likely to be surprised by the second. Raise the question, Why is the derivative stretched vertically? As one explanation, you might have students draw corresponding "rise over run" triangles for both $y = \cos x$ and $y = \cos(2x)$. They can see that while the rise does not change, the run for the compressed graph is half is wide. Thus, the ratio of rise over run is twice as big. In particular, at $x = \frac{\pi}{2}$, the function $y = \cos x$ has a

tangent line with a slope of -1, while at $x = \frac{\pi}{4}$, the function $y = \cos(2x)$ has a

tangent line with a slope of -2. The diagram here shows the tangent lines (dashed) and the "rise over run" triangles:

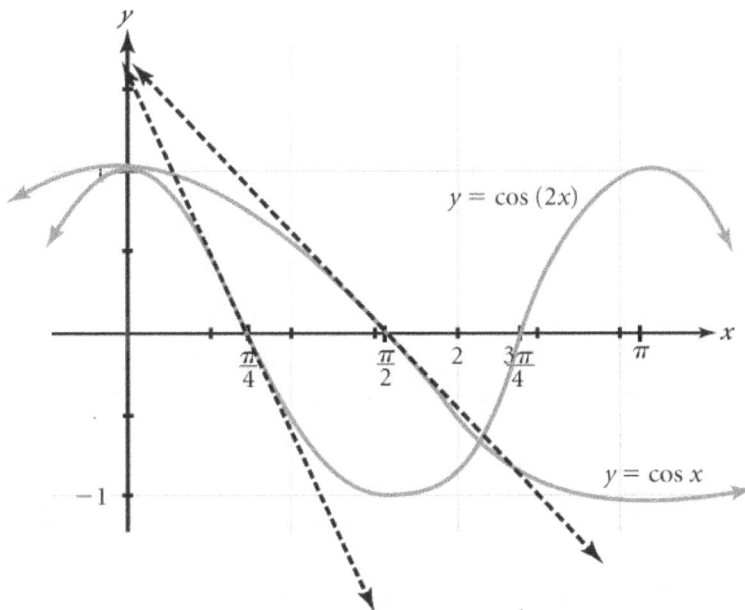

Thus, students have established the following conclusion:

If $f(x) = \cos(2x)$, then $f'(x) = -2 \sin(2x)$.

Bring out that there's nothing special about the particular coefficient 2, and ask, **What function will have a derivative involving** $\sin\left(\dfrac{\pi}{12}t\right)$? Students should note the following:

$$\text{If } f(x) = \cos\left(\frac{\pi}{12}x\right), \text{ then } f'(x) = -\frac{\pi}{12}\sin\left(\frac{\pi}{12}x\right).$$

To eliminate the negative sign in the conclusion, put one in for *f*. Thus,

$$\text{If } f(x) = -\cos\left(\frac{\pi}{12}x\right), \text{ then } f'(x) = \frac{\pi}{12}\sin\left(\frac{\pi}{12}x\right).$$

Completing the Solar Problem

The final step is to replace the new "outside coefficient" of $\dfrac{\pi}{12}$ with 2400. Ask students how to do this, and they will probably see that they can multiply the starting function by $\dfrac{12}{\pi}$ to get rid of $\dfrac{\pi}{12}$ and then multiply by 2400. Thus,

$$\text{If } f(x) = 2400 \cdot \frac{12}{\pi} \cdot -\cos\left(\frac{\pi}{12}x\right), \text{ then } f'(x) = 2400 \cdot \sin\left(\frac{\pi}{12}x\right).$$

This simplifies to

$$f(x) = -\frac{28,800}{\pi} \cdot \cos\left(\frac{\pi}{12}x\right)$$

This is *an* antiderivative, but not necessarily the one we want. The accumulation needs to start at 0. In other words, we need a function that has the value 0 at $t = 0$. To get this, we need to add a (positive or negative) constant to *f*. We calculate that $f(0) = -\dfrac{28,800}{\pi} \cdot \cos 0$, but $\cos 0 = 1$. Thus, $f(0) = \dfrac{28,800}{\pi}$, so we need to add its opposite to the function *f* to get the desired antiderivative.

Thus, the desired antiderivative of the power function $P(t)$ is:

$$E(t) = -\frac{28,800}{\pi} \cdot \cos\left(\frac{\pi}{12}t\right) + \frac{28,800}{\pi}$$

This might be rewritten as

$$E(t) = \frac{28,800}{\pi} \left[1 - \cos\left(\frac{\pi}{12}t\right) \right]$$

How Does It Compare?

As a final step, have students use this function to find the total energy accumulated for the day. They should recognize that they want $E(12)$. We have $\cos\left(\frac{\pi}{12} \cdot 12\right) =$ $\cos \pi = -1$, so $E(12) = \frac{28,800}{\pi} \cdot 2$, which is approximately 18,335 (in watt-hours).

In other words, the solar energy system collects approximately 18.3 kilowatt-hours during the day. The estimate found in *Total Heat* was 18.4 kilowatt-hours, which is amazingly close!

Key Questions

What function might have as its derivative sin $(2x)$?
How is the graph of $y = \cos (2x)$ related to the graph of $y = \cos x$?
Why is the derivative stretched vertically?

Supplemental Activity

Widget Wisdom (extension) gives students an additional example, in an industrial-productivity context, of the effects of the parameters a and b on the derivative of $y = a\ f(bx)$.

A Solar Summary

Intent

Students reflect upon the development of the solution for the solar energy problem.

Mathematics

Students summarize their work on the solar energy problem, describing the steps involved in solving the problem and the role of derivatives and antiderivatives.

Progression

Students describe how they solved the solar energy problem, including how they applied the concepts of derivatives, antiderivatives, and trigonometric functions.

Approximate Time

30 minutes for activity (at home or in class)
10 minutes for discussion

Classroom Organization

Individuals, followed by whole-class discussion

Doing the Activity

This activity requires no introduction.

Discussing and Debriefing the Activity

Use the discussion of students' explanations both to reinforce the fundamental relationship between rate of growth and amount of accumulation and to identify key techniques of differentiation and antidifferentiation that were involved in analyzing the solar energy problem.

"How Much? How Fast?" Portfolio

Intent

Students reflect upon the unit's key concepts as they compile their unit portfolios and write their cover letters.

Mathematics

In the portfolio activity, students focus on the relationship between rate graphs and accumulation graphs and upon the manner in which derivatives and antiderivatives of trigonometric functions were developed in order to solve the solar energy problem.

Progression

Students select activities for inclusion in their unit portfolios and write their cover letters summarizing the unit.

Approximate Time

30 to 40 minutes for activity (at home or in class)
10 to 15 minutes for discussion

Classroom Organization

Individuals, followed by whole-class discussion

Doing the Activity

Have students read the instructions in the student book carefully.

Discussing and Debriefing the Activity

You may want to have students share their cover letters as a way to start a summary discussion of the unit. Then let them brainstorm ideas of what they have learned in this unit. This is a good opportunity to review terminology and to place this unit in a broader mathematics context.

Blackline Master

Zero to Sixty

Speed (in feet per second)

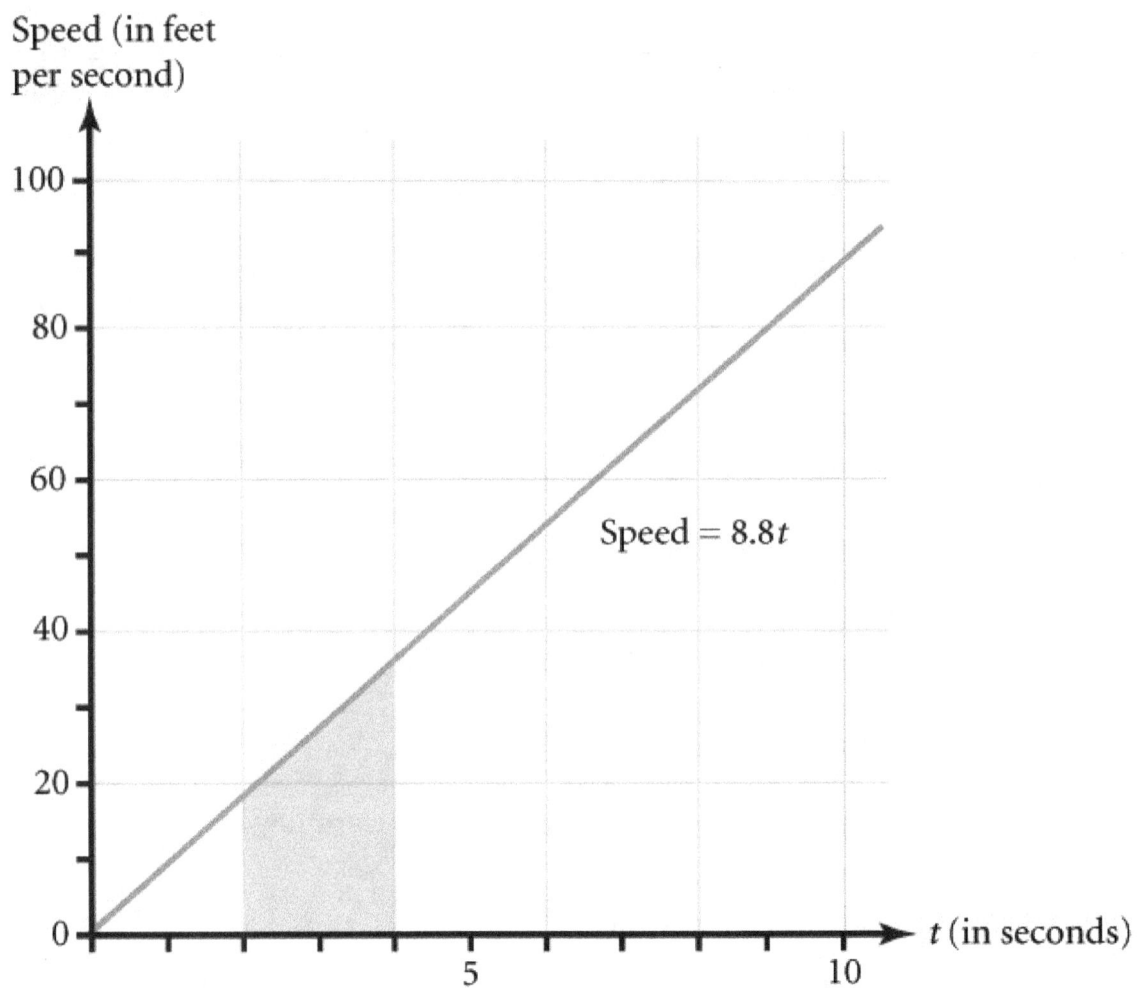

Speed $= 8.8t$

t (in seconds)

¼-*Inch Graph Paper*

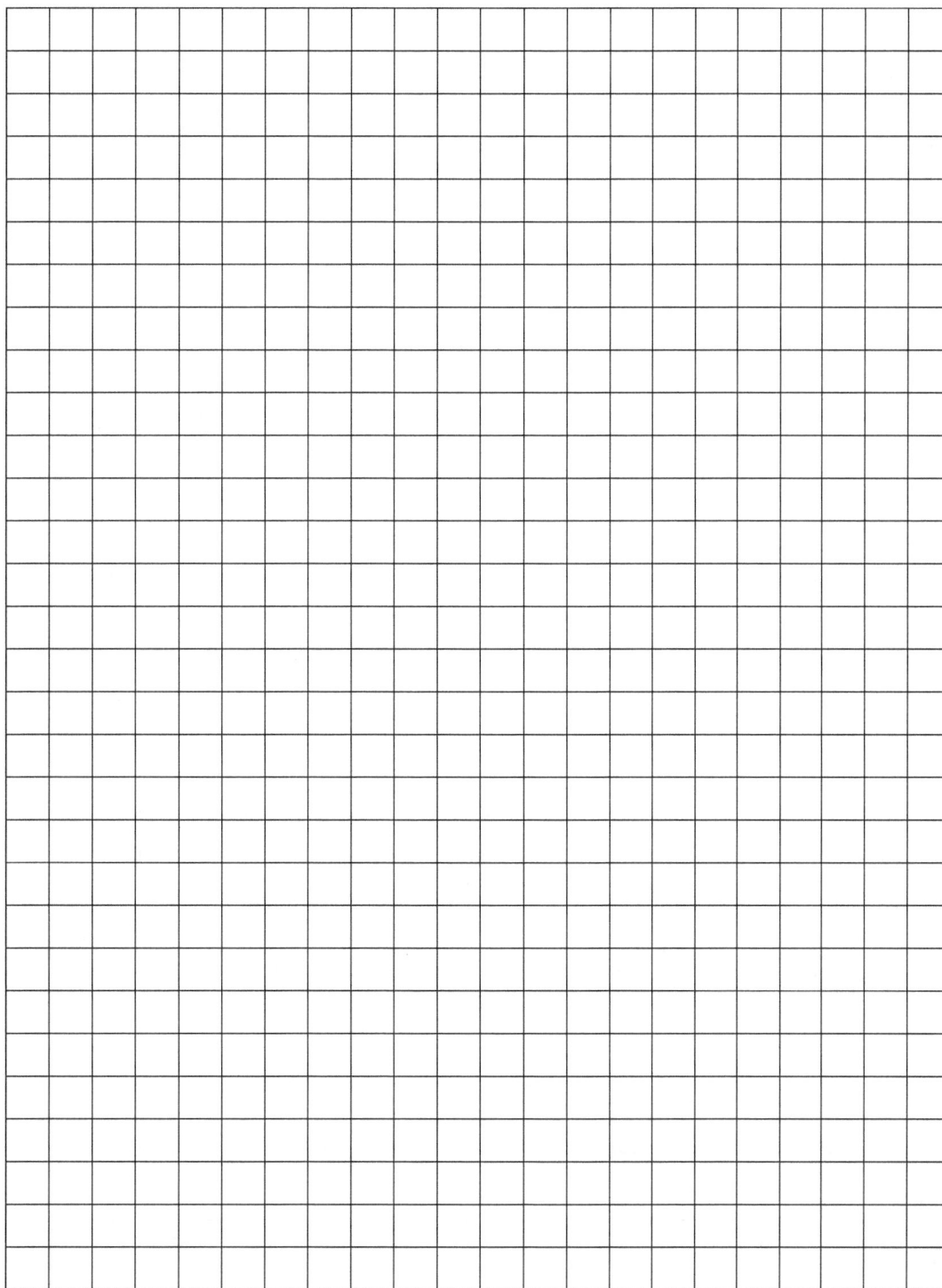

1-Centimeter Graph Paper

1-Inch Graph Paper

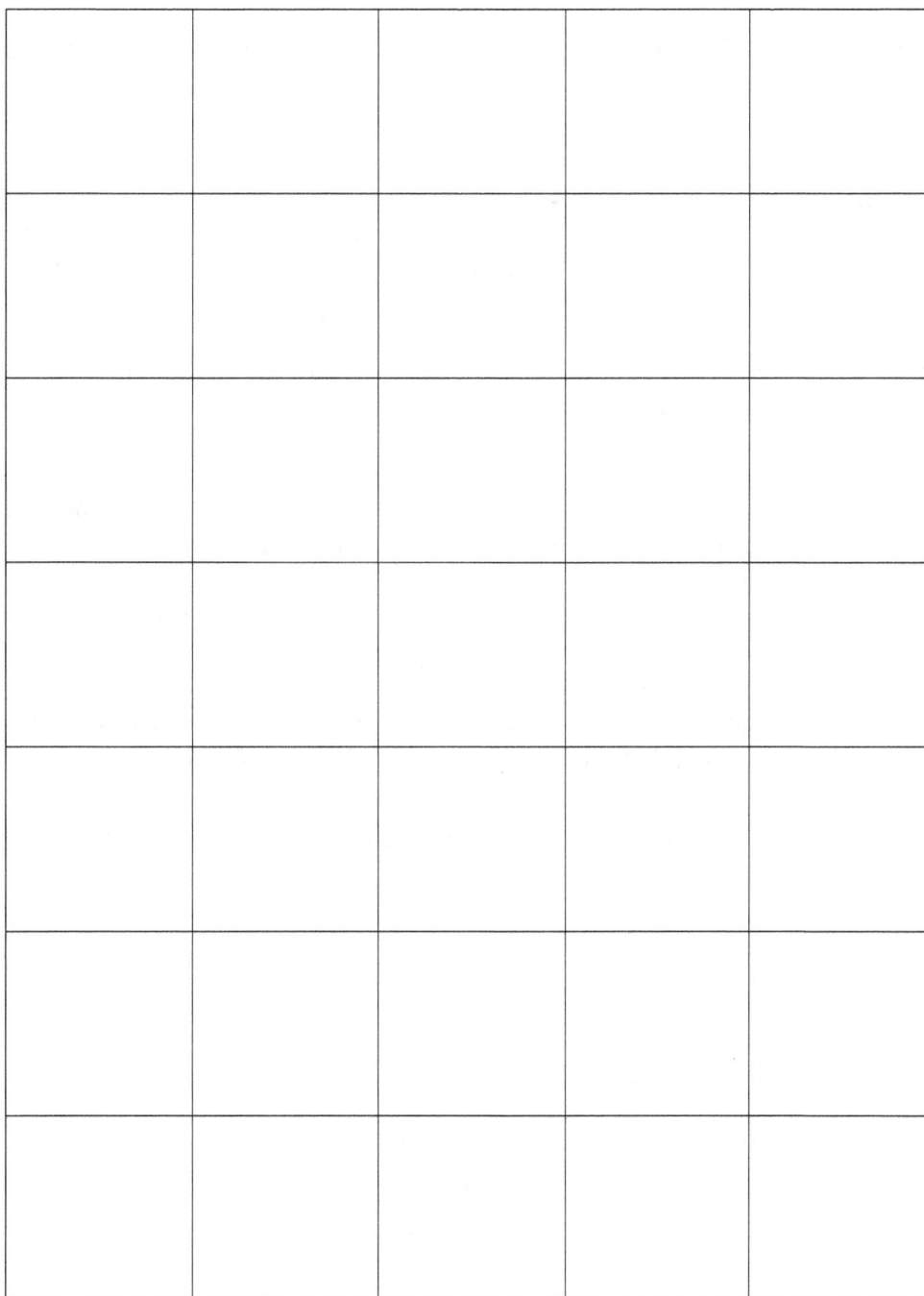

Assessments

In-Class Assessment

1. Find an antiderivative for each function. Use $F(x)$ to represent the antiderivative.

   a. $y = 12x^3 - x^2 + 2x - 5$

   b. $y = 4.32 \cos x$

2. Choose one of the functions from Question 1 and find another antiderivative for it.

3. A car begins moving from a stoplight at time $t = 0$. Its speed for the first 10 seconds is given by the function $s(t) = 0.6t^2$, where t is measured in seconds and s in feet per second.

   a. Find a function $a(t)$ describing the car's acceleration at any time t during this 10-second interval. Explain why your function is correct.

   b. Find a function $d(t)$ describing the distance the car has traveled up to time t. Explain why your function is correct.

   c. Find the car's acceleration, speed, and distance traveled 5 seconds after it began moving. Attach proper units to each of your answers.

4. Explain how to find the value of $\sin\left(\dfrac{3\pi}{2}\right)$ without using a calculator.

1. The diagram shows a portion of the graph of the function defined by the equation $y = x^3 - 2x^2 + 10$.

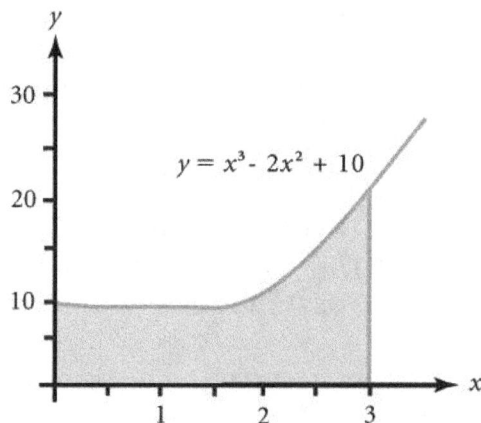

a. Without using any ideas about calculus, *estimate* the shaded area.

b. Explain how you can use ideas about derivatives and antiderivatives to find the shaded area. Give this area exactly.

2. a. Sketch one cycle of the graph of the equation $y = 3 \cos (2x)$ using radian measure.

b. Find the derivative of this function at the point $\left(\frac{\pi}{4}, 0\right)$. Explain how you found this value.

I. *The Pollster's Dilemma*

1. A pollster wants to have a 95% confidence level with at most a 5% margin of error. How many people need to be polled?

2. Explain the role of standard deviation in the statement from Question 1 that the pollster "wants to have a 95% confidence level with at most a 5% margin of error."

3. A poll of 250 voters shows that 175 support a certain proposition. Using the mathematical ideas of *The Pollster's Dilemma,* what can you conclude? State clearly any assumptions you make.

II. *How Much? How Fast?*

1. The general cubic polynomial function is $f(x) = ax^3 + bx^2 + cx + d$, where a, b, c, and d are constants.

   a. Find the derivative of f.

   b. Find the antiderivative of f in its most general form.

2. a. Sketch the graph of the function $g(x) = x^3$ from $x = 0$ to $x = 2$.

   b. Use your sketch to estimate the area under the graph from $x = 0$ to $x = 2$.

   c. Use the equation to find the exact area.

   d. Explain why these two methods yield approximately the same result.

   e. Use your sketch to estimate the rate at which g is increasing when $x = 1.5$.

   f. Use the equation to find the exact rate of increase of g at $x = 1.5$.

III. *As the Cube Turns*

Imagine that your calculator screen is like the face of a clock with only a second hand. Think of the center of the clock and of the screen as the point (0, 0).

If the second hand were pointing to 12, the clock might look something like this:

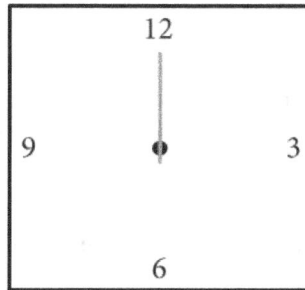

Your task is to write a program that shows the second hand turning. However, your screen will have an *x*-axis and a *y*-axis on it, with (0, 0) at the center.

In addition, your screen won't have the clock numbers or the dot in the center where the second hand is attached. Also, when the second hand is pointing straight up or down or straight to the right or left, you won't see the second hand because it will overlap with one of the axes. So, after the hand is pointing straight up, your next few screens should look something like these diagrams:

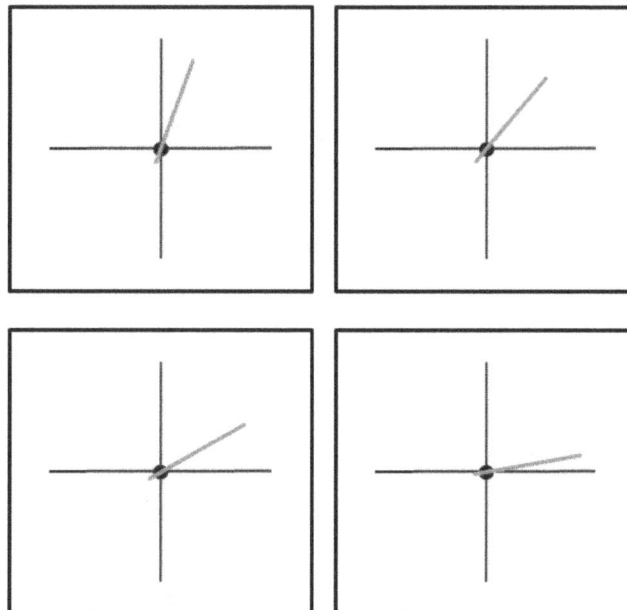

The sequence of diagrams should continue like this, as if the second hand is moving around the center of the screen.

Follow these guidelines:
- Use a window setting in which the scales on the *x*- and *y*-axes are the same.
- Assume that when the second hand is pointing to 12, it is the line segment from (0, −1) to (0, 5).
- Have the second hand make two complete turns around the clock.

You will need to decide these things:
- How many degrees should each turn of the second hand be?
- How long a delay should there be between screens?

As an extra challenge, try to adjust the amount of each turn and the time of each delay so that it actually takes a minute for the hand to go all the way around.

How Much? How Fast? Calculator Guide for the TI-83/84 Family of Calculators

How Much? How Fast? is a largely graphical and numerical introduction to integrals. Many of the scenarios presented in this unit do not have equations attached; students look at graphs and estimate values, slopes, and areas. They use this information to create new graphs or perform calculations. The primary benefit provided by the calculator in this unit will be to facilitate repetitive calculations, for example, to find the distance traveled in a given 1 second, 0.1 second, and 0.01 second period.

There are no Calculator Notes for students for this unit.

Building the Pyramid: To calculate the sum $100^2 + 99^2 + 98^2 + ... + 2^2 + 1^2$ quickly with a calculator, students can sum a sequence of values of X^2 for X from 1 to 100. The command to do this is **sum(seq(X^2,X,1,100,1)**. To find **sum(**, press 2ND [LIST], arrow right to MATH, and select **5:sum(**. To find **seq(**, press 2ND [LIST], arrow right to OPS, and select **5:seq(**.

Let it Fall!: The calculator can help in doing the repetitive work of finding the average speed during the last 2 seconds, 1 second, 0.1 second, and so on, and identifying a pattern or limiting value. One way to ease the calculation is to type the expression on the home screen and press ENTER to calculate, then press 2ND [ENTRY] to recall the expression, and edit to perform the next calculation. You can also use the Y= screen and TABLE feature as shown, with the table set to **ASK,** to find multiple values of an expression quickly.

(16*5²−16*3²)/(5−3)	Plot1 Plot2 Plot3	X	Y₁	Y₂
128	\Y₁■16X²	3	144	128
(16*5²−16*4²)/(5−4)	\Y₂■(Y₁(5)−Y₁(X))/(5−X)	4	256	144
144	\Y₃=	4.9	384.16	158.4
(16*5²−16*4.9²)/(5−4.9)	\Y₄=	4.99	398.4	159.84
	\Y₅=	4.999	399.84	159.98
	\Y₆=	4.9999	399.98	160
		X=		

Trying a New Angle: To do the Application problems, students will need to recall how to change their calculators between degree and radian mode, and will need to remember to do so when needed. Press MODE, highlight the desired elements, and press 2ND [QUIT] to return to the Home screen.

A Solar Formula: Students may want to graph their equation to confirm that it gives the right graph; make sure they use radian mode! They'll need to be careful to enter the equation correctly. $P = 2400 \sin\left(\frac{\pi}{12}t\right)$ is most clearly entered as **y=2400*sin((π/12)*x)).**